D1481976

REMEMBERING AND REPEATING BIBLICAL CREATION IN *PARADISE LOST*

He took the golden Compasses, prepar'd
In God's Eternal store, to circumscribe
This Universe, and all created things:
One foot he centred, and the other turn'd
Round through the vast profundity obscure,
And said, Thus far extend, thus far thy bounds,
This by thy just Circumference, O World.

Paradise Lost, VII. 225–31

The Ancient of Days, or *God Creating
the World*, by William Blake, 1794

REMEMBERING AND REPEATING

BIBLICAL CREATION IN
PARADISE LOST

REGINA M. SCHWARTZ

Associate Professor of English, Duke University

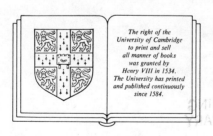

The right of the
University of Cambridge
to print and sell
all manner of books
was granted by
Henry VIII in 1534.
The University has printed
and published continuously
since 1584.

CAMBRIDGE UNIVERSITY PRESS

Cambridge
New York   New Rochelle   Melbourne   Sydney

Published by the Press Syndicate of the University of Cambridge
The Pitt Building, Trumpington Street, Cambridge CB2 1RP
32 East 57th Street, New York, NY 10022, USA
10 Stamford Road, Oakleigh, Melbourne 3166, Australia

First published 1988

Printed in Great Britain at the University Press, Cambridge

British Library cataloguing in publication data

Schwartz, Regina M.
Remembering and repeating: Biblical
creation in *Paradise Lost*.
1. Poetry in English. Milton, John,
1608–1674. *Paradise Lost* – Critical studies
I. Title
821'.4

Library of Congress cataloguing in publication data

Schwartz, Regina M.
Remembering and repeating: Biblical creation in *Paradise Lost*
Regina M. Schwartz.
p.   cm.
Bibliography.
Includes index.
ISBN 0 521 34357 7
1. Milton. John, 1608–1674. *Paradise Lost*. 2. Bible in
literature. 3. Creation in literature. 4. Creation – Biblical
teaching. I. Title.
PR3562. S35   1988
821'.4 – dc19   88-2556   CIP

ISBN 0 521 34357 7

To I. L. Schwartz, Rosanne, and Bart

CONTENTS

Acknowledgments   *page* ix

Introduction
    Repeating   1
    Remembering   3

1 ''And the sea was no more'':
  Chaos vs. creation   8
    The unclean realm   11
    Cosmogonic conflict   24
    Chaos and the fall   31

2 ''Secret gaze or open admiration'':
  The invitation to origins   40
    Curiosity and knowledge   41
    Things visible to mortal sight   53

3 ''Remember and tell over'':
  Creation in sacred song   60
    Ritual recompense   66
    Cosmic liturgy   77
    Paradise Lost as hymn   83

4 ''Yet once more'':
  Re-creation, repetition, and return   91
    The two falls   91
    The Satanic will   94
    Adamic return   103

Notes   111
Works cited   129
Index   137

ACKNOWLEDGMENTS

In a book concerned with the ritual commemoration of gratitude, I am especially grateful for having many debts to remember. William Kerrigan's compelling vision of Milton first inspired me to want to become a Miltonist, and his sustained guidance has made that ambition possible. James Nohrnberg's reading of the Bible has had a deep effect on my own. I appreciate the close attention of others who also read the entire manuscript: the suggestions of Paul Cantor and Jonathan Post have been extremely helpful, and the irreverent comments of James Kincaid saved me from many an overstatement. Louis Martz offered the kind of sympathetic reading I hoped for from distinguished Miltonists. Colleagues and friends who lent support along the way include Florence Amomoto, Mieke Bal, Wayne Cozart, Barbara Fox, Elizabeth Goldman, David Loewenstein, Chester McMullen, David McWhirter, Keith Thomas, James Turner, and Eric White. Like them, John Stevenson managed to say all the right things at all the right times. If the contributions of James S. Ackerman and the late E. Talbot Donaldson are less direct, they are no less essential: this could not be without them.

I want to thank the Milton Society of America for granting the first chapter the James Holly Hanford Award for best Milton article. It was first published in *ELH*, summer, 1985, as "Milton's Hostile Chaos: And the Sea Was No More," and is reprinted here with their permission. A Woodrow Wilson Foundation Charlotte Newcombe Fellowship facilitated the initial drafts, and a generous faculty grant from the University of Colorado allowed time for revision. Lisa Schmidt and Naomi Wood were my tireless research assistants. Kevin Taylor, of Cambridge University Press, has helped this project through each stage of production. Finally, William A. Davis has participated fully in the chaos and the creation of this project, and, remarkably enough, keeps coming back for more.

Boulder, Colorado 1987

INTRODUCTION

Whoever considers the few radical positions which the Scriptures
afforded him, will wonder by what energetick operation he expanded
them to such extent, and ramified them to so much variety ...
                              Samuel Johnson, *Milton*

REPEATING

Milton was preoccupied with origins. He wrote of the origin of the
cosmos, the birth of his god, the birth of the first man and the first
woman, the first utterance, the first interpretation, the first temptation, the first rebellion, the first home, and the first exile. And he
did so by returning to the work he regarded as the first of texts, the
Bible, and, even then, to its beginning, Genesis. His appropriation
of Biblical tradition was hardly inhibiting. Even as he invoked the
Muse of Sinai, he made the most radical claim for innovation
possible: to pursue "Things unattempted yet in Prose or Rhyme."
And yet for all of his preoccupation with origins, Milton approached
the subject uneasily in *Paradise Lost*. There, he is not certain that
beginnings are accessible, and, if they are, he is not sure that they
can be expressed guiltlessly. His creation stories are always mediated
– by accounts and accounts of accounts – by Raphael, by Uriel,
by angelic hymns, by the reconstructions of memory, and by a theory
that casts doubt on the ability of language to convey origins at all.
Milton does not even depict the cosmic creation as a privileged
beginning, a single event that occurred once-upon-a-time and for all
time. Rather, his notion of beginning, like Said's, is that "beginning
is basically an activity which ultimately implies return and repetition
rather than simply linear accomplishment."[1] With chaos continually threatening, creation must be perpetually reasserted. For Milton,
every act is an act of origin, and, conversely, the original act is an
iteration.[2]

1

Introduction

For all of his sympathy with postmodern thought on the iterative nature of origins, Milton's source is Biblical.[3] The creation does not occur once-and-for-all in Genesis. While waters are first parted to create the cosmos, they are parted again at the Red Sea to create a people, and again at the Jordan to signal the creation of the nation. In many ways, the creation narrative is an inappropriate beginning for the Hebrew Bible; Exodus offers a far more likely beginning for the historical vision that dominates it.[4] In fact, in light of ancient Israel's emphasis on historical redemption and her corollary polemic against the creation-fertility myths of neighboring cults, it is remarkable that the Biblical canon includes a creation narrative at all. The oldest credo of ancient Israel, Deuteronomy 26:5–9, omits an account of creation altogether, and composition history teaches that the creation narrative of Genesis 1 is a late addition. Nonetheless, ancient Israel chose not to forgo a creation narrative. Instead, her solution, and her genius, was to obviate any contradiction by assimilating the creation account to her history: the God who created the nation also created the world – both are redemptive acts. As Gerhard von Rad phrased it, the creation was written backwards, from the standpoint of the exodus.[5] Two conclusions emerge. First, Biblical creation is bound fundamentally to the Bible's central myth of liberation, to the exodus from bondage; an origin does not tyrannically dictate an end. Second, to speak of Biblical origin at all, we would speak more accurately of Biblical origin*s*. The Bible offers Milton a model of repeated beginnings.

In the opening invocation to *Paradise Lost*, where Milton is so concerned with first things, he has deferred the first words of the Bible. Instead of beginning "In the beginning ...," he begins with the fall and only then does he proceed to the account of creation.[6]

> Of Man's First Disobedience and the Fruit
> Of that Forbidden Tree, whose mortal taste
> Brought Death into the World, and all our woe,
> With loss of *Eden*, till one greater Man
> Restore us, and regain the blissful Seat,
> Sing Heav'nly Muse, that on the secret top
> Of *Horeb*, or of *Sinai*, didst inspire
> That Shepherd, who first taught the chosen Seed,
> *In the Beginning how the Heav'ns and Earth*
> *Rose out of Chaos*
> (I. 1–10, my emphasis)

This inversion of the apparent Biblical order of creation and fall obtains throughout the poem: only after we meet the fallen angels in Books I and II do we hear Uriel's account of creation in Book III; the war in heaven and fall of the rebel host in Book VI is followed by Raphael's creation account in Book VII; and the fall of Adam and Eve in Books IX and X is followed by Michael's disclosure of the new creation in the final books of the poem. This large structural principle is writ small throughout *Paradise Lost*. Light repeatedly infuses plagues of darkness, and the exoduses follow the exiles. Satan's journey through the darkness of chaos brings him to the precincts of the sun and issues in Milton's invocation to light. Eve's nightmare gives way to an aubade. Even Satan's nocturnal designs of rebellion are quelled in the "morning" in heaven. But once we are attentive to the redemptive character of Biblical creation – its deep structure – it becomes clear that Milton's order only seems to depart from the Bible; instead, he is a most attentive reader, for in the Bible, a recurring pattern of chaos/order (fall/creation) describes an ongoing process of re-creation. Geoffrey Hartman writes that God's knowledge that creation will outlive Sin and Death is expressed so indirectly in *Paradise Lost* (he focuses on extended similes) that it forms a kind of counterplot. "For it does not often work on the reader as independent theme or subplot, but lodges in the vital parts of the overt action, emerging from it like good from evil."[7] In the course of this study, I will make the workings of that counterplot explicit.

REMEMBERING

Repeating is linked to remembering in the Bible, where both assume the sacred context of ritual commemoration. Such commemoration does not begin after an event; rather, ritual repetition becomes part of the event itself. In Exodus, the narration of the Israelites' departure from Egypt is interrupted abruptly – when they are just on the verge of their escape – to prescribe the ritual celebration of the events to follow. The exodus has not yet concluded when the command is given that it must be annually commemorated in the Passover. This ritualization of the event even as it occurs – this building-in of repetition in the first instance – is also evident in the Priestly creation account. The relation between text, utterance, and ritual is an especially rich one in Genesis 1:1–2:4a: the days of the creation comprise a ritual calendar, each marked by the repetitive, "and it was good," a phrase whose ritual force is much like "amen." The final day narrates, not just the creation of another feature of the cosmos, but the creation of the sabbath, that is, the *commemoration*

3

of the events of the prior six days. That sabbath does not stand *apart* from the creation, thereby commemorating an original act; the prescription to repeat and remember the creation is *part of the creation*. Without that provision for ritualized repetition, the creation itself would be incomplete. There would be no seventh day.

Milton was fascinated by this ritualization of the event in the event. In *De Doctrina Christiana* (I. x) he indulges in his own composition history, imagining some editorial patchwork by Moses in order to stress – up front, in Genesis, rather than later, in the Law – the commemorative function of the sabbath. "As for the Sabbath, it is clear that God sanctified it as his own, *in memory of the completion of his task*, and dedicated it to rest''; Milton then directs us to Genesis 2:2–3 and Exodus 31:17: "Six days shall work be done, but the seventh day is a sabbath of solemn rest, holy to the Lord; .... It is a sign for ever between me and the people of Israel that in six days the Lord made heaven and earth, and on the seventh day he rested, and was refreshed" (Ex. 31:15–17).[8] Milton's interest in this verse that enjoins the Israelites to remember is keen enough to prompt several more interpretive maneuvers: noting the illogic of commemorating the creation to Israelites before there are Israelites, Milton is troubled enough to elaborate an explanation.

> But it is not known, because there is nothing about it in scripture, whether this was ever disclosed to Adam or whether any commandment about the observance of the Sabbath existed before the giving of the Law on Mount Sinai, let alone before the fall of man. Probably Moses, who seems to have written the book of Genesis long after the giving of the law, inserted this sentence from the fourth commandment [in Exodus] in what was, as it were, an opportune place [the Priestly creation narrative]. Thus he seized an opportunity of *reminding* the people about the reason, which was, so to speak, topical at this point in his narrative, but which God had really given many years later to show why he wanted the Sabbath to be observed by his people, with whom he had at long last made a solemn covenant.
>
> (*CP*, 6, 353–54, my emphasis)[9]

Milton says that a reason for the sabbath has been assigned by God, to commemorate; that Moses, intuiting the spirit of that reasoning, moved the verse to enable the Israelites to remember better; and that Milton, intuiting the import of remembering in the scripture, has been able to reconstruct Moses' reasons for moving that verse (if he did). This interest in the Biblical commemoration of creation also assumed poetic shape: as the Bible ritualizes the creation in the sabbath, so Milton's account makes the same provision: in Book VII of *Paradise Lost*, the work of each day is celebrated with a complete angelic worship service.

Introduction

Remembering becomes the explicit subject of Deuteronomy (literally, the second or duplicate law). A second Moses enjoins the Israelites to remember the events of the exodus, and he proceeds to repeat that story – a second time – a repetition designed to inscribe the memory of what is to be remembered on his hearers.[10] As Moses retells the exodus, he asks that the Israelites similarly retell those events to subsequent generations. This commemoration is not simply retrospective; it is also forward-looking, for Israel's future is at stake in that memory.

> And these words which I command you this day shall be upon your heart; and you shall teach them diligently to your children, and shall talk of them when you sit in your house, and when you walk by the way, and when you lie down, and when you rise .... And when the Lord your God brings you into the land which he swore to your fathers, ... with great and goodly cities, which you did not build, and houses full of all good things, which you did not fill, and cisterns hewn out, which you did not hew, and vineyards and olive trees, which you did not plant, and when you eat and are full, then take heed lest you forget the Lord, who brought you out of ... bondage ... lest the anger of the Lord your God be kindled against you, and he destroy you from off the face of the earth. (Deut. 6:6–15)

The stark juxtaposition of the promise of Israel's plenty with the threat of complete annihilation is interrupted only by the injunction not to forget.

The Deuteronomic logic of memory informs *Paradise Lost*, where Satan offers the temptation to forget, and to forget the Creator, the Redeemer, is to fall. Satan's question haunts a poem persistently engaged in inquiring into origins: "who saw / When this creation was? remember'st thou / Thy making, while the Maker gave thee being?" (V. 856–58). If it is countered, it is by Raphael's injunction to Adam, "remember, and fear to transgress" (VI. 912), a warning he delivers after he has rehearsed his narrative of creation. As another second Moses, Milton joins the Deuteronomic Moses in remembering the past to redeem the future, punctuating his epic with both the injunction to remember and the rehearsal of the creation to be remembered. "A grateful recollection of the divine goodness is the first of human obligations; and extraordinary favors demand more solemn and devout acknowledgments" (Hughes, 817) opens the *Defensio Secunda*. And in *Ad Patrem*, Milton begins by despairing that he can never repay his father's gift of life, but he concludes consoled that he can "remember and tell over" his kindnesses. His epic would fulfill that promise to his Heavenly Father.

I begin, in the first chapter, with the cosmogonic repetition, offering it as a paradigm of a chaos that continually threatens and a creation that must be perpetually reasserted. In the next two chapters, I turn from the cosmic to the poetic creation where the threat of chaos also prevails. Chapter 2 concerns the poet's access to origins. Milton reformulates that problem, veering away from how to seek an objectified creation, whether "out there" or "back then," to the posture of the seeker. An imperial motive for inquiry – research that would possess its object – leads only to the return of chaos. When knowledge of creation is sought to praise, rather than to possess it, that celebration issues in further re-creations. In the third chapter, I turn to the expression of creation. Ritual commemoration of creation, like keeping the sabbath, keeps chaos at bay. But the ritual force of Milton's sacred song is never assured. If Milton wants to confer his language with performative power, he must contend with the difficulties of interpretation that attend such performance. In the last chapter I address the subject of repetition itself. I contrast ritual repetition of the creation with a repetition that is opposed to creation, pathological repetition. If ritual inscribes memory, mere repetition, like Blake's "same dull round," is predicated upon forgetting. Satan's stubborn will to reenact his battle with substitutes entraps him in an endless cycle he cannot escape. In contrast, Adamic repetition is repetition with a difference, one that can not only accommodate innovation, but is built upon the difference implied by memory – the admission of the pastness of the past.

A book that began as an effort to distinguish pathological from ritual repetition soon became suspicious of the entire enterprise of distinction-making, one which has, in one form or another, dominated Milton criticism for many decades. Among the more prominent distinctions we inherit are between Milton's "intention" and his "practice": whenever a contradiction is noted between these constructs, Milton has been indicted for being unable to maintain consistency. Despite his plan (which many claim access to), Milton created a tyrannizing God; despite his plan, Milton created an attractive Satan. There have also been more sophisticated approaches to distinction-making. As an instrument of education, the poem teaches the reader how to make distinctions, conferring that lesson in subtle and complicated ways that include wrong choices.[11] But, for all of this critical commitment to the notion of Milton's "poetry of choice,"[12] Milton himself tells us that opposites constitute one another. Good and evil are twin-born; the knowledge of them both is "involved and interwoven," "the matter of them both is the same," he tells us in *Areopagitica*. And so, while I begin this book

Introduction

with a fundamental opposition, between creation and chaos, and make it my paradigm for other distinctions – between licit and illicit knowledge, language that ritually performs and language that cannot, ritual and pathological repetition – all of those distinctions break down in the face of the *continual* struggle between oppositions. ''Alternatives'' may never clarify themselves into a choice at all; rather, the poem may offer at all moments the possibility of both. If cosmos must repeatedly defeat chaos, it is because chaos inheres in it. In the Babylonian account of creation, the heavens and the earth are formed from the divided body of the chaos monster, Tiamat; and in Genesis 1, the original waters of chaos, Tehom, are divided by the firmament to create the world. To understand the logic of an iterative creative act is ultimately to understand that creation and chaos are so ''involved and interwoven'' that they constitute one another. The unspoken temptation of *Paradise Lost* may be to assume that its options achieve resolution, when, instead, they poise us ever on the brink of the clarity choice offers – so very tantalizingly.

1

"AND THE SEA WAS NO MORE": CHAOS VS. CREATION

> The angels fell; man's soul fell; and their fall shows us what a deep chasm of darkness would still have engulfed the whole spiritual creation if you had not said at the beginning *"Let there be light"; and the light began.*
> Augustine, *Confessions*

Milton the theologian is as emphatic and unambiguous as he could be on the subject of a good chaos.

> This original matter was not an evil thing, nor to be thought of as worthless: it was good, and it contained the seeds of all subsequent good. It was a substance, and could only have been derived from the source of all substance. It was in a confused and disordered state at first, but afterwards God made it ordered and beautiful. (*CP*, 6, 308)

He goes on to anticipate the objection that, lacking form, such a first matter must have been imperfect: "But in fact, matter was not, by nature, imperfect. The addition of forms (which, incidentally, are themselves material) did not make it more perfect but only more beautiful." In Milton's cosmos, all proceeds from God, a good God; hence, all – including first matter – must be good.

> O *Adam*, one Almighty is, from whom
> All things proceed, and up to him return,
> If not deprav'd from good, created all
> Such to perfection, one first matter all ...
> (V. 469–72)

Milton argues for a good chaos with good reason. Not only is it consistent with his materialistic cosmos, it is vital to the success of his theodicy. An evil chaos would indict, rather than justify a God from whom all proceeds, accusing him of fashioning a universe rotten at its very core. Then, too, any intimation of an evil creative act would soon plunge Milton into the mire of Gnostic thinking so antithetical to his own cosmology that it suggests Blake's radical revision instead. Milton's creation is no "fall" into base materialism; it is an emanation of divine goodness. He even substitutes the theory of creation *de Deo* for the orthodox doctrine of creation *ex nihilo* to safeguard its goodness.[1]

If the author of an evil chaos were not God, the implications would be equally heretical: an evil principle coeternal with God suggests dualism at worst; at best, some hedge upon divine omnipotence. But we know Milton to be an avowed and consistent monist. Meric Casaubon (1599 – 1671) thought that the devil introduced to men the common mistakes concerning the origin of evil, prominent among them "that God is not omnipotent, and wanted not will, but power to amend what they conceived to be amiss in the world: or, that there were two Authors and Creators of all things, the one good, and the other evill ... For, said they, were God as omnipotent, as he is good, why hath he not made all things as goodnesse would have prompted?"[2] With no less than the justice, oneness, and omnipotence of God at stake, Milton's position on the nature of chaos is no arcane piece of cosmological speculation. Rather, it is with the greatest care that he must deliberately and explicitly assert the goodness of first matter.

There is, nonetheless, a dark side to even his most confident assertions. Raphael's definitive-sounding discourse on cosmic perfection finesses the problem of evil, relegating it unobtrusively to the passive voice. All is perfect if not "deprav'd from good." This must be among the most troubling uses of the passive in the poem: "deprav'd" by whom, given that all proceeds from God; and how and why is such a corruption of a perfect creation even possible? Here, in the most explicit doctrine of a perfect world, the possibility of its corruption still lurks. We are offered a creation that cannot be evil but can become evil, as mysteriously as that agentless passive. Just how far back to seek the source of that corruption – whether in the fall of man, of Satan, in a flawed creation, or in the Creator himself – is the hard question the epic both invites and silences.

A cosmological explanation for the problem of evil has not been the primary approach of Christianity. Instead, it has focused on man's fall and on the redemption from the fall made possible by divine mercy. Seeking the origin of evil in the universe itself invites the kinds of questions Casaubon attributes to the devil, with dualism prominent among them. Augustine, the theologian who does inquire into the cosmological dimension, offers a solution that preserves both God's goodness and his omnipotence: evil is privation. But Milton's uncompromising monism leads him to suspect latent dualism even here, to wonder if Augustine has not merely substituted "nothing" for evil as a second principle. A.S.P. Woodhouse tells us that Milton's doctrine of a good first matter turns him away from the "avowed dualism of the Platonic tradition, and the concealed dualism of the Augustinian, to a form of monism." With that insistence upon a single good substrate of all things, Woodhouse claims, Milton "cuts away the cosmological groundwork of ... evil, ... sacrific[ing] the Christian solution of the problem of evil on the cosmological level."[3] I would suggest that, on the contrary, it is precisely to this level that Milton's inquiry leads him. In his quest for beginnings – "Say first," he implores the Muse of Creation, "say first what cause / Mov'd our Grand Parents in that happy state, / Favor'd of Heaven so highly, to fall off" (I. 28–30) – Milton is thrust back again and again to *the* beginning. And for all its disturbing implications, the chaos he finds there is far more hostile than he would ever acknowledge in prose. Despite his doctrine of a good chaos, his poem depicts a very different one: a region that is "waste and wild" and an allegorical figure who claims that "havoc and spoil and ruin are my gain."

Impressive scholarly excavation has been done on the subject of Milton's chaos, searching out its rightful place in tradition. A.B. Chambers has explored Milton's debt to classical antiquity and A.S.P. Woodhouse has located it in its Neoplatonic context, but surprisingly little has been written about the imaginative place of chaos in Milton's poem itself.[4] By and large, scholars have taken their cue from *De Doctrina Christiana*, accepting Milton's word on the goodness of first matter. When they have peered into the chaos of the epic, they have found it, at worst, neutral. Robert M. Adams tells us that "Chaos is neutral as between good and evil; all he likes is disorder. That inclines him to evil, of course, but not all the way, for evil is itself a principle of order; and Chaos is, so to speak, beyond good and evil."[5] Even so, Adams is apparently drawn toward another conclusion, one he rejects only on the grounds that evil must be "organized." But far from being ordered, evil is the very violation of order in *Paradise Lost*, with Satan himself the harbinger of disorder. He promises to turn the new world over to chaos and his "designs" of imperialism degenerate into the upheaval of mountains in heaven. Satan's protean nature – clouded angel, good cherub, toad, cormorant, serpent – is reminiscent of the "unstable visage" of the Anarch, Chaos, and the Adversary's countenance (or one of them) is distorted by chaotic passions on Mt. Niphates. Michael Lieb also finds chaos itself neutral: "The Abyss is not inherently evil, although it can be put to evil use.

Nor is it inherently good, although it can be put to fruitful use."
God finds in it "the womb of nature" while for Satan it is "a
grave."[6] Even this depiction of chaos, as a pliable realm definable
only by interpretation, is not true to the destructive, threatening
region described in the poem. Chambers shows a greater awareness
of the hostility of chaos, especially in his conclusion: "Chaos is as
true an exemplar as hell of that state which everywhere prevails when
the laws of providence are set aside, when the ways of God to man
are opposed and overturned."[7] Nonetheless, his essentially scientific
approach to the composition of first matter reduces a would-be active
threat into the safety of a remote principle. Woodhouse tentatively
concedes the possibility that chaos may be evil, consigning the
observation to a footnote – a remarkable footnote to be sure, one
which runs against the grain of his (and Milton's) entire argument
in favor of a good first matter:

It must, for example, be plain to every reader of *Paradise Lost* that the
description of the Chaos there throws a very much heavier emphasis on its
formlessness and disorder than does the account of the original matter in
the *De Doctrina*, so that it is difficult to escape the inference, denied in the
treatise, that this disorder is, or at all events has some affinity with, evil.[8]

I find the inference of an evil chaos so difficult to escape that it is
not worth trying. Instead, I plan to plunge into this dark abyss and
search, amid its very confusion, for some resolution of the conflict
between Milton's doctrine and depiction, for the place allotted chaos
in Milton's theodicy.

THE UNCLEAN REALM

In *Paradise Lost*, Milton depicts the creation as the act of delimiting,
of setting bounds.

                    ride forth, and bid the Deep
    Within appointed bounds be Heav'n and Earth.
                                        (VII. 166–67)

    He took the golden Compasses, prepar'd
    In God's Eternal store, to circumscribe
    This Universe, and all created things:
    One foot he centred, and the other turn'd
    Round through the vast profundity obscure,
    And said, Thus far extend, thus far thy bounds,
    This be thy just Circumference, O World.
                                        (VII. 225–31)

In this, Milton adheres to the Bible, where the Priestly account of Genesis I describes creation as a series of separations. God divides the light from the darkness, he separates the waters above the firmament from the waters below, and he divides the dry land from the sea. One rabbinic commentator insists that the Hebrew verb for "to create," *bara*, stems from "to cut."[9] Others add the image of the compass to Proverbs 8:27, underscoring the sense of delimiting: "When he established the heavens, I was there, when he drew a circle on the face of the deep." Rashi describes the circle on the deep as "a great limit that could not be over-run."[10]

The divisions of creation are only the beginning of distinction-making in the Bible. "Hallowing begins," according to Ernst Cassirer, "when a specific zone is detached from space as a whole, when it is distinguished from other zones and one might say religiously hedged around."[11] What is sacred is what is set apart; Milton's garden with its high walls, the holy ground Moses stands on, Jerusalem, the Temple, and heaven itself are all marked off by thresholds. Israel is hallowed, for it is drawn from among the nations, a people set apart. As God says to Moses, "And you shall be holy unto me for I the Lord am holy, and have separated you from the peoples, that you should be mine" (Lev. 20:26). The Hebrew root for "holy" also means separated, cut off, whereas "profane" means open for common use.[12] One scrupulous translator has even rendered the commandment, "Be Holy for I am Holy":

> I am the Lord your God, who rescued you from the land of Egypt;
> I am set apart and you must be set apart like me.[13]

The creation is sanctified by its divisions. As the Bible repeatedly tells us, they are "very good."

In contrast, Milton's chaos is virtually "defined" by its lack of definition, its limitlessness. In that "immeasurable" abyss – not yet measured by the golden compasses – all of the categories of time, place, and dimension established at creation are missing. Chaos is an

> Illimitable Ocean without bound,
> Without dimension, where length, breadth, and highth,
> And time and place are lost.   (II. 891–93)

As the divisions that mark creation are "good," their absence suggests the opposite. The classical tradition seconds this Biblical verdict on the unbounded. For the Pythagoreans and Plato "limit and the unlimited ... are set off against each other as the determinant and the indeterminant, form and formlessness, good and evil.''[14] Plotinus tells us to think of evil ''by thinking of measurelessness as opposed to measure, of the unbounded against the bound, the unshaped against the principle of shape.'' His expanded definition of evil is strikingly applicable to Milton's chaos:

[T]hink of the ever-undefined, the never at rest, the all-accepting but never suited, utter dearth; ... whatsoever fragment of it be taken, that part is all lawless void, while whatever participates in it and resembles it becomes evil .... Evil is that kind whose place is below all the patterns, forms, shapes, measurements, and limits, that which has no trace of good by any title of its own but (at best) takes order and grace from some principle outside itself.[15]

Certainly Milton's chaos cannot claim any title to good of its own; it is only when God ''puts forth his goodness'' that chaos becomes the material of creation. Milton's ever-warring ''lawless void'' is also never at rest, and the evil that ''participates in and resembles'' chaos most is Satan, the breaker of all bounds.

To classical and Biblical precedent, we can add Milton's own depiction of the perils of boundlessness, a judgment made on his own grounds. In his material universe, where ''from the root / Springs lighter the green stalk, from thence the leaves / More aery, last the bright consummate flow'r / Spirits odorous breathes'' (V. 479–82), moral categories tend to assume physical shape. Boundaries take on far more than physical significance. The sacred space of Paradise is delimited by no less than four natural walls (IV. 131–47); nonetheless, Satan ''At one slight bound high overleap'd all bound'' (IV. 181) – a rich adumbration of his every action in the poem. When Gabriel apprehends Satan, he rebukes him:

> Why hast thou, Satan, broke the bounds prescrib'd
> To thy transgressions, and disturb'd the charge
> Of others, who approve not to transgress
> By thy example, but have power and right
> To question thy bold entrance on this place;
>
> (IV. 878–82)

Dense with allusion to bound-breaking, this passage includes references to each of Satan's transgressions: the first, when he ''broke peace in Heav'n and Faith, till then / Unbrok'n'' (II. 690–91); the second, when he breaks through hell's gates of ''burning Adamant'' which ''Barr'd over us prohibit all egress'' (II. 436–37); his latest violation of Paradise and a fourth that Gabriel piously refuses, to transgress the command to stay Satan. Throughout these and its

13

many other uses in the poem, "transgress" carries its literal meaning, "to step over," and, in turn, "unbounded" carries its moral significance, to transgress. So the "boundless continent" of the Paradise of Fools will be inhabited by transgressors of various kinds. With the fall, the world is "fenceless," Death "stuffs" a "vast unhide-bound Corpse," and hell can no longer hold Sin and Death "in her bounds." Most striking is Satan's own confession that his ambition to reign in heaven is an "unbounded hope." Literally unbounded, we might add, for that ambition seeks to break the bounds of hierarchy. In Milton's world, to violate bounds is to fall.

With this emphasis on boundaries, Milton subscribes to that rich category of thinking on the sacred and profane, pollution and purity, that informs Biblical thought. As the creation is first hallowed by separations, so it is remembered and sanctified by observing those original distinctions. Leviticus tells us that it is written to "put difference between holy and unholy, and between unclean and clean" (Lev. 10:10, AV). In parallel structural studies, Mary Douglas and Jean Soler have demonstrated that the force of Israel's dietary laws with their seemingly recondite distinctions (why should the frog be clean and the hare unclean?) is just that: to preserve the distinctions made at the Beginning, to keep holiness inviolate.[16] "Every time a Jew eats," according to Soler, "he remembers the Creation." A fish that crawls (shellfish), a bird that walks (the stork), an animal that flies (insects) – any creature that violates its category is unclean, for such creatures violate no less than world order. "They are unclean because they are unthinkable." Because God made each thing "according to its kind," man must not mix what God has separated.

You shall not sow your field with two kinds of seed;
Nor shall there come upon you a garment of cloth made of two kinds of stuff.
(Lev. 19:19)

All hybrids and confusions are abominated. Furthermore, the sanctity of life – God blesses life at creation – makes death unclean. Neither high priest nor Nazirite can go near a dead body (Lev. 21:11, Num. 6:6 – 7), one of the vows Samson violates when he eats honey from the carcass of the dead lion. Deriving sustenance from the dead is a macabre confusion of life and death. Separating them pays homage to life, to creation, to the Creator.

A poet committed to distinction-making, who repeatedly dramatizes that most difficult separation of good from evil, "culling and sorting asunder" truth from falsehood, is clearly drawn to the

Bible's own emphasis on distinctions. Mary Douglas' observation is as applicable to Milton as it is to the Bible:

Defilement is never an isolated event. It cannot occur except in view of a systematic ordering of ideas ... the only way in which pollution ideas make sense is in reference to a total structure of thought whose key-stone boundaries, margins and internal lines are held in relation by rituals of separation.[17]

Virtually all of the significant action of *Paradise Lost* is conceived with reference to these categories. The poem centers on the distinction between forbidden and permitted food. An ur-dietary law governs Paradise.[18] Like the later injunctions of Leviticus, the force of that first law is not simply to forbid, to exact obedience, but to commemorate and sanctify the creation. In that law, Paradise is given a constant reminder of the Maker. Its violation is accompanied by a lapse of memory: Eve addresses the serpent as her author. Adam's first words to his faded flower are a lamenting reminder – too late – of the gift of life she has forgotten and thereby forsaken: "O fairest of Creation, last and best / Of all God's Works ..." (IX. 896–97). Furthermore, obedience to the law is tacit assent to the very notion of lawgiver and receiver, an acknowledgment of the most fundamental of Biblical distinctions – between the Creator and his creation, between the Maker and his work. To transgress the law is not only to forget, but to effect the most heinous of confusions, aspiring, as Eve does, to become "as the Gods." Such ambition is "unclean," and it is expressed, appropriately enough, in terms of Biblical pollution. When Eve eats the forbidden fruit, she commits the most abhorred of abominations: "eating Death," that "mortal taste." The grim image recurs in the Thyestian banquet simile at the fall. Satan's scorn of his easy seduction of man –

> Him by fraud I have seduc'd
> From his Creator, and the more to increase
> Your wonder, with an Apple   (X. 485–87)

– stems from one who has long ago denied that all-important distinction between Creator and creation, one who is "sustained" by the doubly unclean diet of apples turned to ashes.

Creaturely categories are violated by a talking snake and Leviticus even singles out the serpent for special censure: "Every swarming thing that swarms upon the earth is an abomination.... You shall not make yourselves abominable with any swarming thing that swarms; and you shall not defile yourselves with them, lest you become unclean" (11:41–43). Swarming things are particularly unclean because their mode of locomotion is unclear; they neither swim, walk, nor fly and so they fail to belong in either sea, land, or air. As serpent alone, Satan is unfit for creation. He understands his own descent into a serpent as a fall from pure to mixed, from holy to unclean.

> O foul descent! that I who erst contended
> With Gods to sit the highest, am now constrain'd
> Into a Beast, and mixt with bestial slime,
> This essence to incarnate and imbrute,
> That to the highth of Deity aspir'd;
> But what will not Ambition and Revenge
> Descend to? (IX. 163–69)

To the irony of his ascent leading to a descent, Satan adds the self-awareness that his unclean ambition to violate "his kind" and sit with the highest results in this unclean mixture with a beast. As his ambition issues in revenge, so one mixture gives rise to another. His anti-creative goal is to "mingle and involve" earth with hell, and the bridge Sin and Death build between them does literally break their bounds. Appropriately, the providential design frustrates that effort in like terms. Those sent by Satan to pollute are ultimately employed in the divine service to clean. Sin and Death will "lick up the draff and filth / Which man's polluting Sin with taint hath shed / On what was pure" and heaven will be restored forever "To sanctity that shall receive no stain" (X. 629–31; 39). The fall of the unclean angels only results in the purification of heaven.

> Then shall thy Saints unmixt, and from th' impure
> Far separate ... sing. (VI. 743–44)

In the banquet scene of *Paradise Regained*, Satan offers Jesus unclean food, asserting that he has the right to all created things (*PR*, II. 320–28). Jesus refuses on the grounds that this giver is unacceptable. In his study of the scene, Michael Fixler concludes that Milton is thereby rejecting the dietary prohibitions of Leviticus:

such detailed ritualistic prohibitions as are enjoined in *Leviticus* xi would have for him no positive force as expressing the everlasting will of God. Moreover, there is an indication here that any assumption restricting Man's free will and faith by chaining piety or virtue to such injunctions would act as an instrument of temptation. The danger latent in these laws, when considered as absolute commandments, becomes apparent when Satan deliberately assumes that their prohibitive force is still binding upon Jesus.[19]

When he considers these laws as "absolute commandments," Fixler fails to distinguish – as Milton invites us to – between the two contrary senses of the term "bounds." Those that shackle the will,

16

that mark legalism, are anathema to this spokesman for freedom. But when the will is perceived not as the passive recipient of binding, but as the active force that binds, it replicates the divine creative act of separating, distinguishing – Miltonic choosing. Jesus' criterion of purity – its dependence upon the nature of the giver – is true to the spirit informing the dietary laws: to remember the Giver.

This imagery of pollution naturally attaches itself to Milton's boundless region. Chaos is unclean. The elements distinguished at creation are confounded here.

> Of neither Sea, nor Shore, nor Air, nor Fire,
> But all these in thir pregnant causes mixt
> Confus'dly ...   (II. 912–14)

Its mixtures and confusions violate all laws of sanctity and its embryon atoms "swarm populous." This unclean substance, "neither Sea / Nor good dry Land"[20] (Milton reminds us of the goodness of distinctions), elicits unclean locomotion. Satan "tread[s]" the "crude consistence, half on foot, / Half flying":

>   So eagerly the fiend
> O'er bog or steep, through strait, rough, dense, or rare,
> With head, hands, wings, or feet pursues his way,
> And swims or sinks, or wades, or creeps, or flies ...
>   (II. 947–50)

So too, when Satan appears on the outer shell of the created universe, he discovers a "windy Sea of Land," the Paradise of Fools, which has obvious affinities to chaos. Here wings must be used to move across land, as in "*Sericana*, where Chineses drive / With Sails and Wind their cany Waggons light" (III. 438–39), and here, where the distinctions of creation do not hold, only the "unaccomplisht works of Nature's hand, / Abortive, monstrous, or unkindly mixt" (III. 455–56) can live. Satan is particularly at home. Julia Kristeva has distinguished two basic positions of Biblical impurity. Either (1) impurity is a force outside of and threatening divinity or (2) it is intrinsically dependent upon divine will – what is impure is whatever departs from divine precepts.[21] Milton draws power from both, as we shall see. In the resolution of these seemingly conflicting notions of impurity – an outside force, but one subsumed to the will of God – we find the same logic that will inform Milton's chaos. It is a chaos that is hostile, an "Other," but one which God has created. Ultimately, subsuming this Other, evil, to divinity is the project of his theodicy.

17

The violation of categories is not simply abhorrent; it is dangerous. Anthropologists offer another model for approaching the unbounded, demonstrating that the absence of meaningful social boundaries threatens identity itself. In his classic study of rites of passage, Arnold van Gennep first isolated the stages marking these rituals: separation, transition, and incorporation.[22] Drawing upon his work, Victor Turner has focused on the middle term, the transitional or "liminal" stage the neophyte must endure once he has disengaged from one role and before he has fully assumed his new one.[23] This inherently unstable position is a "no man's land" without clearly definable boundaries – like Milton's chaos. Because liminal states defy definition, they are marked by their ambivalence. "Undoing, dissolution, decomposition are accompanied by processes of growth, transformation, and ... reformulation ... logically antithetical processes of death and growth may be represented by the same tokens, for example, huts and tunnels that are at once wombs and tombs." The single most memorable description of Milton's chaos is as "the Womb of nature and perhaps her Grave" (II. 911). Both contraries are potential in chaos. Turner adds that "Liminality may perhaps be regarded as the Nay to all positive structural assertions, but as in some sense the source of them all, and, more than that, as a realm of pure possibility."

Undoubtedly, it is this ambivalence that has given rise to the prevailing critical assumption that Milton's chaos is neutral. But potential does not always carry positive connotations: Henry More wrote that matter is "the lowest and last ground of all things ... a mere potentiality."[24] And for a poet preoccupied with the moment of choice, one who depicts the crisis of decision before temptation in his four major works, this state of indecision, of being neither one thing nor the other, cannot be neutral. Indeterminacy – I think again of the unstable visage of the Anarch, Chaos – may well pose a greater threat in Milton's moral universe than the Satanic one of a definite willed disobedience. Robert M. Adams has even gone so far as to suggest that Satan and God are allied in *Paradise Lost* against their common enemy, Chaos. With God, Satan defines the moral universe, clarifies the choice. The real mire is failure to choose, weakness, chaos. "For a poet whose epic aspirations call for him to make his way across vast physical and imaginative distances, to organize immense bodies of material, to poise a fictive world in the void, the figure of Chaos could represent an authentic psychic menace."[25] Indeterminacy does not have to suggest moral ambiguity.

Chaos vs. creation

The negative side of the liminal chaos looms larger as its association with death, decay, and dissolution grows more insistent in the
poem. This uncreated ill-defined place (or no-place), somewhere in
between the identifiable regions of heaven and hell, threatens others
with loss of identity. In contrast to his vague intimations about earth
(II. 443–44), Satan shows an uncanny awareness of chaos before
he has ever journeyed there. ''Long is the way and hard'' through
the gates of hell;

> These past, if any pass, the void profound
> Of unessential Night receives him next
> Wide gaping, and with utter loss of being
> Threatens him, plung'd in that abortive gulf.
>
> (II. 438–41)

Here we find the kinds of epithets most frequently attached to chaos:
an aborted birth, a womb that miscarries, a void which threatens
with ''utter loss of being.'' When he objects to the doctrine of creation
ex nihilo in *De Doctrina*, Milton tells us, with Lear, that nothing can
come of nothing. Nonetheless, his chaos owes a far heavier debt to
the Augustinian understanding of evil as privation than he would
ever acknowledge in prose. With ''havoc, spoil, and ruin'' his gain,
the Anarch's is a kind of negative empire, made vast by destruction.
It is as Nothing that chaos will be most threatening.

Satan's intuitive grasp of the void is not accidental; they share a
certain sympathy. The only encounter Chaos has in the poem is with
Satan, whose journeys through the abyss – at his fall from heaven,
en route to tempt man, and upon returning to hell to announce his
victory – make it familiar territory. Needless to say, such dark mis-
sions also color chaos by association. I would revise Adams' alliances
to suggest that Satan suffers a predicament far more like chaos than
not. As it is a liminal region, he is a liminal figure. Angels expelled
from heaven are, so to speak, ''structurally invisible,'' homeless,
banished from the presence of God like the chaos God has aban-
doned. Having lost their positive identity, they have lost their names,
yet another characteristic of liminality.

> Though of thir Names in heav'nly Records now
> Be no memorial, blotted out and ras'd
> By their Rebellion, from the Books of Life.
> Nor had they yet among the Sons of *Eve*
> Got them new Names ...   (I. 361–65)

Disguises are another hallmark of such figures, and in the course of
Satan's transformations it becomes clear that disguises do not simply

19

mask identity; they rob it. Even when his form had not yet lost "All her original brightness," Satan is taken aback: "If thou beest he; But O how fall'n! how chang'd / From him, who ... didst outshine / Myriads though bright" (I. 84 – 87). How much greater the disfiguration as Satan heaps further damnation upon himself. Significantly, only Chaos has no trouble recognizing him (II. 990).

Like liminal figures who are "neither living nor dead from one aspect and both living and dead from another,"[26] Satan suffers a death in life rather like Coleridge's grisly Mariner. Despite their boast that "this empyreal substance cannot fail," the fallen angels make just that failure one of their main themes during the debate in hell. Moloch imagines that an "enrag'd" Deity

> Will either quite consume us, and reduce
> To nothing this essential, happier far
> Than miserable to have eternal being:
> Or if our substance be indeed Divine,
> And cannot cease to be, we are at worst
> On this side nothing ... (II. 96 – 101)

Moloch's doubts of their immortality – "*if* our substance be indeed Divine" – are seconded, but far more eloquently, by Belial, in an infernal version of Hamlet's soliloquy:

> To be no more; sad cure; for who would lose,
> Though full of pain, this intellectual being,
> Those thoughts that wander through Eternity,
> To perish rather, swallow'd up and lost
> In the wide womb of uncreated night,
> Devoid of sense and motion? ... (II. 146 – 51)

Given the fundamental tenet of angelology, the invulnerability and immortality of the "pure Intelligential substances," this is a peculiar discussion indeed. Both miss the irony of debating over open war – considering its possible dangers and consequences – when that war has been fought and the consequences, including being swallowed up in the wide womb of uncreated night, are already upon them. (That irony does not escape Beelzebub, who turns it to his ends: "What sit we then projecting peace and war? / War hath determin'd us, and foil'd with loss / Irreparable;" [II. 329 – 31].) Even as they suffer, they have also, in a sense, ceased to be. When Satan first conceives his rebellion, Abdiel spurns him with a reference to one of the most fantastic of Biblical episodes: the rebellion of Korah, when the envious sons of Levi murmur against the authority of Moses and Aaron:

Yet not for thy advice or threats I fly
These wicked Tents devoted, lest the wrath
Impendent, raging into sudden flame
Distinguish not: for soon expect to feel
His thunder on thy head, devouring fire.   (V. 889–93)

Korah and his men become types of Satanic presumption, and their horrible fate is shared by Satan and his host. "Depart, I pray you," Moses warns the congregation, "from the tents of these wicked men, and touch nothing of theirs, lest you be swept away with all their sins."

"If these men die the common death of all men, or if they are visited by the fate of all men, then the Lord has not sent me. But if the Lord creates something new, and the ground opens its mouth and swallows them up, with all that belongs to them, and they go down alive in to Sheol, then you shall know that these men have despised the Lord." And as he finished speaking all these words, the ground under them split asunder; and the earth opened its mouth and swallowed them up .... So they ... went down alive into Sheol.   (Num. 16:29–33)

Here, as in *Paradise Lost*, non-being is not simply an ontological category; it is a moral judgment. Death is the offspring of Sin.

Ultimately, the void of Chaos and the loss of identity of Satan are rooted in a common source, and in Miltonic fashion, that source is a decision. Both deny creation. Both are "Adverse to life."

That we were form'd then say'st thou? and the work
Of secondary hands, by task transferr'd
From Father to his Son? strange point and new!
Doctrine which we would know whence learnt: who saw
When this creation was? remember'st thou
Thy making, while the Maker gave thee being?
We know no time when we were not as now;
Know none before us, self-begot, self-rais'd
By our own quick'ning power ....   (V. 853–61)

If we were to isolate a single moment as Satan's fall – although his degeneration is more accurately spoken of as a process – it would be here. For once Satan denies his origin, he determines his end, as Abdiel foresees with chilling clarity.

O alienate from God, O Spirit accurst,
Forsak'n of all good; I see thy fall
Determin'd ....   (V. 877–79)

This exchange offers one of the most explicit expressions of the relation between the creation and the fall in the poem: the denial of the former issues in the latter. The punishment suits the crime. To deny the Maker is to be unmade.

> Then who created thee lamenting learn,
> When who can uncreate thee thou shalt know.
>
> (V. 894–95)

Without minimizing the significant difference between the willful denial of Satan and the ontological one of chaos, we must, nonetheless, accept the terms of Milton's universe wherein things physical also have a moral life. A kind of Miltonic logic leads us to a conclusion that defies strict logic: chaos is evil because this uncreated realm cannot acknowledge its Creator. I venture into such a radical conclusion with an eye toward Milton's view of the creation. In a real sense, the entire epic constitutes an extended refutation of Satan's heresy of self-begetting. As W. B. C. Watkins has observed, Milton "never lets us forget from beginning to end the Divine creative process. It is both [the] substance and structure of his epic .... Of Milton's great themes Creation is most completely and serenely realized in his work."[27] Milton's structural revision of the original ten books of the epic to twelve makes Raphael's recital the great centerpiece of the poem. And the creation story is not only given prominence of place; Raphael recites these events as part of the divine initiative to warn Adam against the Tempter. Just as to deny the creation is to fall, to remember is to resist. The angel concludes his narrative of the war in heaven and introduces his creation account with the telling warning: "Remember, and fear to transgress." In this veritable hymn to creation, what is uncreated cannot be neutral.

When God creates, "He puts forth his goodness" into an abyss that has need of it, one that is more infernal than indifferent.

> His brooding wings the Spirit of God outspread,
> And vital virtue infus'd, and vital warmth
> Throughout the fluid Mass, but downward purg'd
> The black tartareous cold Infernal dregs
> Adverse to life ....   (VII. 235–39)

In fact, the distinction between chaos and hell is blurred repeatedly in the poem, beginning with the argument to Book I: "then the poem hastes into the midst of things, presenting *Satan with his Angels now fallen into Hell*, describ'd here, *not in the Centre ... but in a place of utter darkness, fitliest call'd* Chaos." When Satan promises to reduce earth to its "original darkness and sway of Chaos," we need not assume (as Empson does[28]) that he is dissembling, intending all the while to erect his own standard of hell there rather than that of ancient Night. Hell and Chaos are allied in the common purpose of havoc, spoil, and ruin. The following description of hell, with its mixtures, its monstrosity, and its living death, could just as well describe chaos:

> O'er many a Frozen, many a Fiery Alp,
> Rocks, Caves, Lakes, Fens, Bogs, Dens and shades of death,
> A Universe of death, which God by curse
> Created evil, for evil only good,
> Where all life dies, death lives, and Nature breeds,
> Perverse, all monstrous, all prodigious things,
> Abominable, inutterable ....   (II. 620–26)

Milton's synonyms for chaos are used interchangeably for hell: the Deep, Void, Gulf, Pit, Waste, and Wild. First peering into hell, Satan "views / The dismal Situation waste and wild" (I. 59–60) – Milton's translation of the Biblical abyss of Genesis 1:2. And when he heaves himself from the infernal waves, he says the thunder "ceases now / To bellow through the vast and boundless Deep" (I. 176–77). Other examples abound, among them: "into what Pit thou seest / From what highth fall'n" (I. 91–92); "all the hollow Deep / Of Hell resounded" (I. 314–15); and "Transfix us to the bottom of this Gulf" (I. 329). Hades and Orcus are members of Chaos's train and Chambers notes that there is classical precedent for their association. For Seneca, Statius, and Ovid, "Chaos was 'deformed,' 'blind,' 'black,' 'Cimmerium,' 'Tartariem,'" and Virgil associates Erebus, Chaos, Hecate, Phlegethon, and "silent places in the wide-spread night."[29]

The Bible also offers Milton what is virtually a generic Deep, at once the primordial waters, the abode of Leviathan, and Sheol, the region of the dead.[30] Then, too, Biblical directions have moral dimension: "to go up" refers to the ascent to the Promised Land, the top of Sinai, and heaven; while "to go down" invariably describes a descent into Egypt, to death, to Sheol.[31] While Milton's chaos lies between heaven and hell, Satan enters the Deep – even from hell – by descending (II. 917–34). In the pseudepigraphal Book of Enoch there is a remarkable description of the place prepared for the fallen angels. It is not hell, but chaos.

And I proceeded to where things were chaotic. And I saw there something horrible: I saw neither a heaven above nor a firmly founded earth, but a place chaotic and horrible. And there I saw seven stars of the Heaven bound together in it, like great mountains and burning with fire .... These are of the number of the stars of heaven which have transgressed the command-ment of the Lord, and are bound here till ten thousand years, the time en-tailed by their sins, are consummated ... and from thence I went to another place which was still more horrible than the former, and I saw a horrible thing: a great fire there which burnt and blazed, and the place was cleft as far as the abyss .... This place is the prison of angels, and here they will be imprisoned forever. (21:1–10)

Finally, Satan himself offers the most powerful expression of their identity. Feeling the "abortive gulf" of chaos within, he describes that internal hell as a devouring Deep.

> Which way I fly is Hell; myself am Hell;
> And in the lowest deep a lower deep
> Still threat'ning to devour me opens wide. (IV. 75–77)

COSMOGONIC CONFLICT

Given all of these explicit identifications of chaos with hell, its league with Satan, its enmity to life, we may well wonder how readers of *Paradise Lost* have managed to neutralize it. Their method is archaeol-ogical. Thus far, I have neglected the description of chaos that has most interested the critics: chaos as warring embryon atoms.

> For hot, cold, moist, and dry, four Champions fierce
> Strive here for Maistry, and to Battle bring
> Thir embryon Atoms; they around the flag
> Of each his Faction, in their several Clans,
> Light-arm'd or heavy, sharp, smooth, swift or slow,
> Swarm populous, unnumber'd as the Sands
> Of *Barca* or *Cyrene's* torrid soil,
> Levied to side with warring Winds, and poise
> Thir lighter wings. To whom these most adhere,
> Hee rules a moment; Chaos Umpire sits,
> And by decision more imbroils the fray
> By which he Reigns: next him high Arbiter
> *Chance* governs all. (II. 898–910)

A critical debate has raged over whether these atoms are Demo-critean, Epicurean, or neither, largely diverting attention from Milton's own chaos.[32] Chambers has conducted an impressive excavation of the atomistic tradition. I quote one passage at length to demonstrate that for all of its impressive learning, the effect of this approach is to tame the fierce enemy of God into a problem of scientific history.

Milton's "embryon atoms" are "swift or slow"; those of Epicurus move all at the same speed .... Milton's chaos has qualities while the atoms themselves do not. Democritus allowed them shape and size; either he or Epicurus added that they have weight. But other qualities they do not possess. Indeed, as Aristotle and Chalcidius pointed out, an insistence upon unqualified first principles was one of the major factors which rendered the atoms of Democritus so recognizably distinct from Anaxagorean particles. And XVII-century atomism clings to this cardinal point; Henry More allows his "parvitudes" extension only. When Milton says that his fierce champions – hot, cold, moist, and dry – "to Battle bring Thir embryon atoms," (II. 899–900), at the very least he indicates that chaos represents a later stage of development than unqualified atoms in space.[33]

Atomism has not always been approached with such cool objectivity. As material mechanism comes to the fore in the seventeenth century, atomism becomes an intensely emotional issue, with Christians abhorring it as an "atheistical doctrine." On Epicurus, Democritus, and Empedocles, Ralph Cudworth is vituperative.[34] And the physician to Charles I, Walter Charleton, voices his sentiment with no equivocation: he isolates Epicurus as "the most notorious Patron, though not the Father of [the] execrable delusion" that the universe was not created by God, but resulted by chance from "an infinite Chaos of Atoms." He then turns on Lucretius who "was deplorably infected with this accurst contagion of Epicurus."[35] Charleton had three major objections to atomism, all seated in a defense against dualism: (1) that a chaos of atoms is believed to be "as ancient as eternity"; (2) that such atoms were not created by God *ex nihilo*; and (3) that blind Fortune, not God, has arranged them. As Du Bartas phrases it:

> Once all was made; not by the hand of *Fortune*
> (As fond *Democritus* did yerst importune.)
>
> (*Divine Weeks*, 2)

To these can be added a fourth, one especially important for Milton. Atomism inverts the entire structure of sacred history. Biblical history begins with order, with a good creation, proceeds through the fall of man to the chaos of human history, and ends with the final restitution of order. According to atomism, random chaos is the first principle, with order following from a fortuitous combination of atoms. Lucretius explains that "after making trial of all kinds of union and motion, those atoms at length unite which suddenly combining, oft become the beginnings of great things, of earth and sea and sky."[36] These bonds just as fortuitously dissolve, giving way to

chaos in the end.[37] Chaos, order, chaos – this atomistic scheme has
its spokesman in *Paradise Lost*. It is Satan's intention to reduce the
world to its "original darkness" and thereby subvert the providential scheme. Like atomism, infernal theology substitutes chance for
providence. But sacred history speaks, not of entropy, but of disobedience; not of the random collision of particles, but of redemption.
Once again, Milton's chaos, even his atomistic chaos, proves
Satanic.

Ultimately, an inquiry into Milton's chaos requires no such extensive recourse to philosophical history. Arnold Stein has remarked
that "One besetting temptation of scholarship is that in its effort to
recover things that have grown dim it may make them too clear."[38]
Such blinding clarity about Milton's intellectual past can cloud his
imaginative present. For the closest analogue to Milton's chaos is not
to be found in tradition at all: it is Milton's own war in heaven.[39]
Chaos not only threatens life, it is also Satanic in its insurgence,
threatening to storm heaven itself. The abyss is churned

> by furious winds
> And surging waves, as Mountains to assault
> Heav'n's highth, and with the Centre mix the Pole.
> (VII. 213–15)

Its noise is as

> if this frame
> Of Heav'n were falling, and these Elements
> In mutiny had from her Axle torn
> The steadfast Earth. (II. 924–27)

These are, above all, *warring* embryons, and this is a *military* chaos,
and that is why Satan can make a league with its commander against
their common enemy, God.

Milton develops the analogy in similes. Passages on chaos in
Book II and on the war in heaven in Book VI seem to be virtually
cross-referenced. As the commotion in chaos is compared to a mutiny
that would tear the earth from her axle, so, during the war, "all
Heav'n / Resounded, and had Earth been then, all Earth / Had to
her Centre shook" (VI. 217–19). Only the time intervening between
the war and Satan's journey through chaos – time enough for the
creation of the earth – distinguishes these passages from one
another. (And to look ahead for a moment, that very reference to
creation in the midst of this anarchy is proleptic of the outcome of
the war.) The "noises loud and ruinous" of chaos are explicitly
compared to war:

> when *Bellona* storms,
> With all her battering Engines bent to rase
> Some Capital City ...   (II. 922 – 24)

And the "horrible discord" familiar to chaos was never known in heaven until the war (VI. 207 – 10). The description of the war in heaven even includes a direct reference to warring elements, the very components of chaos:

> Millions of fierce encount'ring Angels fought
> On either side, the least of whom could wield
> These Elements, and arm him with the force
> Of all thir Regions ...   (VI. 220 – 23)

Raphael tells Adam that the war in heaven is much worse than any hurling of the elements; but elsewhere, when Milton compares the warring elements of chaos with storming a capital city and heaven itself, he interposes the caution that he compares "great things with small" (II. 921 – 22). Neither is the worse war then; the point is that they are obviously comparable. Chance – "the ideological enemy in *Paradise Lost*"[40] – rules the warring elements of chaos and according to Belial, it would take Chance and Chaos to govern a war in heaven, that is, a war that God would lose (II. 232 – 33). In Spenser, the "divelish engin" is wrought in hell (*FQ*, 1.7.13), but Milton's chaos yields up the instrument of war (IV. 482): the "Deep" of heaven is mined for the "Sulphurous and Nitrous" cannonfire (VI. 512 – 20). And when Satan journeys into chaos, he would fall forever through the void were he not stopped by a "tumultuous cloud / Instinct with Fire and Nitre" (II. 936 – 37). It seems that chaos spontaneously forms gunpowder. Finally, the war in heaven threatens the return of chaos. Hills are upheaved and hurled. Rocks, water, and woods are tossed until order degenerates into utter confusion: "horrid confusion heapt / Upon confusion rose" (VI. 668 – 69). Without divine intervention, chaos would have won heaven back (VI. 670).

This close connection between, on the one hand, an insurgent chaos, and, on the other, a war in heaven that collapses into chaos is part of a deeper – and much older – symbolic connection. The war in heaven is generally acknowledged to presage the final battle with Satan at the end of time. Isabel MacCaffrey has noted in another context that in "the logic of return, recovery and remembrance that governs the Judeo-Christian tradition, the war in Heaven, for which Milton found a source in Revelation, is transferred to the beginning."[41] So positioned at the beginning, Milton's war invites comparison to a long tradition of battles at the beginning: the myth of the primordial battle between the Creator-deity and Chaos. In this myth, creation issues from their conflict, for cosmos depends upon the defeat of chaos. While that primordial battle remains tacit in Milton's epic, as it does in the Bible, the suggestion of a cosmogonic conflict is embedded deep in the mythic fiber of *Paradise Lost*. The war in heaven is itself symbolic of that conflict: after all, the war ends in the creation, a creation, we are told, explicitly designed to repair the injury from that war. Then, too, that insistent symbolic equation between the war and chaos suggests that creation not only follows the defeat of Satan; Milton's cosmos depends upon the defeat of that other adversary – Chaos.

The myth of the cosmogonic battle was prevalent throughout the ancient Near East. The *Enuma Elish*, the Babylonian creation account, depicts a struggle between the monster of the primordial waters, Tiamat, who seeks the destruction of the younger gods, and Marduk, their defender. Only when Marduk, armed with the four winds, defeats Tiamat, is he able to establish both divine order – he becomes the king of the gods – and cosmic order. He cuts the slain Tiamat in two, separating the upper waters from the lower waters, and proceeds to create the sun, moon, and stars to regulate the seasons, in an order paralleling that of Genesis 1. After establishing a cosmic "house," Marduk makes provisions for his own house, the temple of Babylon, and finally, he forms man from the blood of the rebel leader – to serve the gods.[42] This defeat of the primeval abyss was not a once-always event: annually, it was believed, the waters of chaos must be pushed back from the dry land, and annually the victory of cosmos over chaos was ritually reenacted. Ugaritic texts portray another conflict between the fierce Sea (Yamm) or River (Nahar) and the storm-deity (Baal).[43]

> Then soars and swoops the mace in the hand of Baal
> Even as an eagle in his fingers.
> It smites the head of Prince Sea,
> Between the eyes of River the Ruler.
> Sea collapses and falls to the ground;
> His strength is impaired
> His dexterity fails.
> Baal drags Sea away and disperses him.
> He annihilates River the Ruler.

Just how deep the Bible's debt to these neighboring myths runs is, as we might expect, a sensitive and much-debated issue,[44] but the fact of their influence is undeniable. The chaos monster is retained in Biblical metaphor in Leviathan and Rahab; and, while the precise connection between these enemies of the Deep and the Adversary, Satan, is difficult to reconstruct,[45] that imaginative connection bridges the Bible from beginning to end. The Bible opens with a reference to the subdued Tiamat, Tehom, the deep over which the spirit of Elohim broods, and it closes with the final defeat of the Dragon, heralding a new heaven and a new earth when the sea shall be no more (Rev. 21:1). In between, the myth has been historicized: the battle is fought for Israel's liberation from human oppressors, for the creation of the nation instead of the cosmos. Leviathan is replaced by Pharaoh and the Deep by the Red Sea.[46] In one of the oldest poems in the Bible, the "Song of the Sea" (Ex. 15:1–18), the exodus is celebrated in terms reminiscent of that primordial conflict; while the explicit enemy is Pharaoh's host, the waters of the Red Sea are also constrained.

The Lord is a man of war; / the Lord is his name. Pharaoh's chariots and his host he cast into the sea; / and his picked officers are sunk in the Red Sea.... At the blast of thy nostrils the waters piled up, / the floods stood in a heap; / and the deeps congealed in the heart of the sea.... Thou didst blow with thy wind, and the sea covered them; / and they sank as lead in the mighty waters. (Ex. 15:3–10)

Allusions to the slaying of the dragon of the Deep grow more insistent in later prophetic references to the exodus. Here, even as Deutero-Isaiah invokes the exodus to herald a new redemption, he describes that exodus in terms of the ancient victory over chaos.

Was it not thou that didst cut Rahab in pieces, that didst pierce the dragon?
Was it not thou that didst dry up the sea, the waters of the great deep;
that didst make the depths of the sea a way for the redeemed to pass over?
And the ransomed of the Lord shall return, and come to Zion with singing;
everlasting joy shall be upon their heads;
they shall obtain joy and gladness,
and sorrow and sighing shall flee away.
(Is. 51:9–11)

The theme reaches its crescendo in apocalyptic literature; only there does it assume its full mythic shape in the Bible. The conflict leaves the human battlefield and enters the cosmic lists. The kingdom of God confronts the kingdom of Satan, and in a final showdown, creation does battle with its old enemy, Chaos.

In that day the Lord with his hard and great and strong sword will punish Leviathan the fleeing serpent, Leviathan the twisting serpent, and he will slay the dragon that is in the sea. (Is. 27:1)

Whether the primordial battle is invoked with reference to creation, the exodus, or the new creation, it signals salvation. In *The Symbolism of Evil*, Paul Ricoeur has isolated the myth of the cosmogonic battle, the "drama of creation" as one of the central myths of the origin of evil. In this scheme, evil is very much a cosmological principle, for "it is the *'chaos' with which the creative act of the god struggles.*" He adds, and each of our Biblical excerpts offers testimony, that "the counterpart of this view of things is that *salvation is identical with creation itself*; the act that founds the world is at the same time the liberating act."[47]

It is here, in Biblical poetry, that our most sensitive reader of the Bible found a model for his chaos, the enemy of the Deep.[48] With the lightest touch, Milton invokes this ancient tradition of the cosmogonic battle, and in a poem professing to justify the ways of God to man, this drama of redemption assumes its rightful place. On the verge of Milton's cosmos, when "the sacred influence / Of light appears," chaos retires "As from her outmost works a brok'n foe" (II. 1034–35; 1039). As Uriel describes the creation, chaos is made to flee like a routed enemy:

> Confusion heard his voice, and wild uproar
> Stood rul'd, stood vast infinitude confin'd;
> Till at his second bidding darkness fled,
> Light shone, and order from disorder sprung:
>
> (III. 710–13)

Raphael's account of creation offers the fullest elaboration of the conflict. Here, the Son rides forth in a chariot with the full equipage of war, leaving the gates of heaven as a warrior would leave the gates of "some capital city" – and all this to create the world.

> Meanwhile the Son
> On his great Expedition now appear'd,
> Girt with Omnipotence, with Radiance crown'd
> Of Majesty Divine, Sapience and Love
> Immense, and all his Father in him shone.
> About his Chariot numberless were pour'd
> Cherub and Seraph, Potentates and Thrones,
> And Virtues, winged Spirits, and Chariots wing'd,
> From the Armory of God, where stand of old
> Myriads between two brazen Mountains lodg'd
> Against a solemn day, harness't at hand,
> Celestial Equipage;
>
> (VII. 192–203)

Chaos vs. creation

The divine army surveys the insurgent enemy:

> They view'd the vast immeasurable Abyss
> Outrageous as a Sea, dark, wasteful, wild,
> Up from the bottom turn'd by furious winds
> And surging waves, as Mountains to assault
> Heav'n's highth, and with the Centre mix the Pole.
>
> (VII. 211–15)

But then, on the very brink of this dire confrontation with chaos, one promising to be more terrible than the clash with Satan in heaven, the conflict – and with it the machinery of martial epic – is completely deflated. The Son has no worthy foe. His Word has no need of arms.

> Silence, ye troubl'd waves, and thou Deep, peace,
> Said then th' Omnific Word, your discord end:
>
> (VII. 216–17)

The stately ease with which the enemy is subdued here is consonant with the opening image in Genesis, where the fierce monster of Babylonian myth, Tiamat, lay vanquished in a mere allusion to Tehom, the quieted deep over which the spirit of God broods. Milton offers another figural hint of the defeat of chaos. Those bronze mountains flanking the chariots and horses of God's armory (VII. 200–1) are a reference to Zachariah's apocalyptic vision. In Milton's scheme, this victory of creation over chaos anticipates the final one "on that solemn day" of judgment. Lodged in the midst of the drama of the Beginning is an allusion to the End. In between, chaos threatens at other confrontations: when Satan and Death nearly come to blows, and when Satan and Gabriel bristle. But these, like all of the battles in *Paradise Lost*, amount to so much shadow-boxing, as Stanley Fish puts it.[49] There is no real contest in a world governed by providence. Leviathan is harnessed easily enough: as it says in Job, the Lord has hooked him like a fish (41:1–2).

CHAOS AND THE FALL

If there has been something like a critical conspiracy to detoxify chaos, there are good reasons for it, reasons that informed Milton's own protest of a good first matter. Once we posit an evil chaos with which the Creator must strive, we open ourselves to those questions insinuated by Meric Casaubon's devil about the omnipotence, oneness, and justice of God. How do we answer this devil? Or, in more

31

scholarly terms, how do we reconcile Milton's explicit doctrine of a good first matter with the hostile chaos portrayed in the epic? What are we to make of this pressing contradiction? Dennis Danielson puts the important theodical questions baldly:

First, what is the connection between the evil of Chaos and that evil which is traceable to human or angelic agency? and secondly, is it possible to cling to any notion of evil ultimately transcending creaturely agency without lapsing into dualism?[50]

I would suggest that the answer to this second problem rests upon the solution to the first, and, in turn, that first question contains the seed of its own answer: the connection between the evil of chaos and human agency.

Ricoeur's response to the relation between primordial evil and the evil of the fall is radical: there is none. Regarding them as two completely different myths of the origin and end of evil, he dissociates the "drama of creation" from the "drama of the fall," asserting that by its very nature, the creation drama excludes the notion of a fall, and, inversely, the idea of a "fall" of man becomes fully developed only in a cosmology from which any creation drama has been eliminated. While salvation is identified with creation itself in the first "mythic type," in the drama of the fall, "salvation is a new peripeteia in relation to the primordial creation; salvation unrolls a new and open history on the basis of a creation already completed and, in that sense, closed."[51] But our poet upsets the philosopher's distinction. Milton joins the Bible in charging the creation with redemption and redemption with creation, the salvation at the end with the salvation at the beginning.[52] For Milton, the primordial battle with chaos becomes symbolic of the human struggle with sin.

As the mythic conflict is largely displaced onto a human struggle in the Bible, so it is in *Paradise Lost* where the battle is fought in the Garden instead of in Egypt. Presumption and ingratitude become Milton's monsters of the deep. Born in the night of Satan's invidious designs and armed in the war in heaven, they are roused again at the Temptation. This connection between human fault and chaos explains why it is not simply described as a realm of confusion: chaos is also depicted as insubordinate and disobedient. To look again at Uriel's creation account, we find him speaking of chaos as "standing ruled," as heeding its master's bidding.

> Confusion heard his voice, and wild uproar
> Stood rul'd, stood vast infinitude confin'd;
> Till at his second bidding darkness fled,
> Light shone, and order from disorder sprung; (III. 710–13)

Milton's version of the *fiat lux* includes a drama of submission. To create is to exact obedience from a recalcitrant, even fallen, chaos.

Not only is chaos fallen; at the fall, chaos is come again, physically, morally, and psychologically.[53] The distinctions that marked creation begin to break down. The four elements once again "strive for maistry."

> To the Winds they set
> Thir corners, when with bluster to confound
> Sea, Air, and Shore, the Thunder when to roll
> With terror through the dark Aereal Hall.   (X. 664–67)

The sun, moon, and stars, originally appointed to ordain the seasons, days and years, steer off their course, and the earth's axis is pushed off-center; "they with labor push'd / Oblique the Centric Globe" (X. 670–71). The center cannot hold. Discord, the first daughter of Sin and the familiar member of Chaos's entourage, reigns on earth as "beast with beast gan war." The dietary regime of Paradise collapses as all devour each other. But the chaos within – the counterpart of the paradise within – is worse still. Adam suffers in a "troubl'd Sea of passion tost" (X. 718), and despair drives him ever deeper into the abyss, echoing Satan's "lowest deep to lower deep."

> O Conscience, into what Abyss of fears
> And horrors has thou driv'n me; out of which
> I find no way, from deep to deeper plung'd!   (X. 842–44)

With the fall, "havoc, spoil, and ruin" triumph.

Logically, a truly evil chaos should ameliorate human fault. Ricoeur speaks of the "terrible possibility" inhering in the cosmogonic myth, that innocent man is born into a flawed world that victimizes him. He perpetrates an evil he discovers, rather than introducing it.[54] But logic has always been a limited guide into the realm of symbols. So long as chaos itself is understood as symbolic of human fault, evil is not removed from human agency to be pushed back to a remote cosmological flaw. Thomas Goodwin shows how thoroughly intertwined the association between cosmic and human evil, between chaos and the fall, had become in the seventeenth century:

Since the fall, our hearts of themselves are nothing but *darknesse*, ... The Apostle compareth this native darknesse of our hearts unto that *Chaos*, and lumpe of *darknesse* which at the first creation *covered the face of the deepe*: when he sayes, that *God who commanded light to shine out of darknes* (hee referreth to the first creation, Gen. 1.1,2.) *hath shined into our hearts* …. And if at any time he withhold *that light* … Then so farre doe our hearts presently returne to their former darknesse: … Darknesse *covereth not the face of this deepe only*, but it is darknes to the bottome, throughout darknesse. No wonder then, if when the *Spirit* ceaseth to *move upon* this *deepe* with beames of light, it cast us into such *deepes* and darknesse.[55]

Furthermore, if we were to deny any connection between the primordial battle and the fall, we would soon find ourselves in the awkward and untenable position of denying any relation between Milton's cosmic battle – the war in heaven – and his human one, in the Garden. The poem would soon fall apart.

The Bible, which has managed to draw power from the myth of a hostile chaos without compromising its doctrine of radical monotheism, offers another key to the connection between cosmogonic evil and human agency. We have already seen that the imagery of the primordial battle surfaces in references to the exodus; a hostile deep also appears in the contexts of apostasy, injustice, and the punishment for "turning away from God." A disobedient Jonah is rebuked in the deep:

> I called to the Lord, out of my distress, and he answered me;
> out of the belly of Sheol I cried, and thou didst hear my voice.
> For thou didst cast me into the deep, into the heart of the seas,
>   and the flood was round about me;
> all thy waves and thy billows passed over me.   (Jonah 2:2–3)

Divine wrath is described as a descent into Sheol:

> Thou hast put me in the depths of the Pit,
>   in the regions dark and deep.
> Thy wrath lies heavy upon me,
>   and thou dost overwhelm me
>   with all thy waves.   (Ps. 88:6–7)

Bernhard Anderson, the same Biblical scholar who traces the extensive references to the cosmogonic battle throughout the Bible in a study tellingly titled *Creation versus Chaos*, also concludes that the evil of the Bible is an evil that comes after creation, corrupting it. He senses no contradiction when he asserts (and he could be speaking of Milton here) that "Evil is the fruit of the freedom of the creature."[56] Brevard Childs adds that while the Bible "struggles to contrast the creation … with an active chaos standing in opposition to the will of God … in the hands of the Priestly writer, the primordial battle becomes a 'broken myth' " invoked for the creation itself. Whether as metaphor, "broken myth," or – as in the Apocalypse – as belief, a hostile chaos becomes a powerful expression of human fault.

This brings us to a contradiction at the heart of the Christian myth of salvation: an omnipotent God has no real enemy, yet the notion of redemption involves the defeat of just such an enemy. Pushing this crux to the limit, the Russian theologian Berdjaev suggests that when we have eradicated any hint of an evil principle, we are left with the absurd vision of salvation history as a game or a play in which, in essence, "God play[s] with Himself."[57] And so, an evil chaos is not "merely" metaphor either; if it were, creation would not truly be redemptive.

It is here, in a redemptive creation, that we find the seeds of reconciliation between Milton's description and his doctrine of chaos. *Felix culpa* is not an after-the-fact rationalization for Milton. We know good by knowing evil. Milton reads the logic of that fortunate fall back into his cosmology: a fallen chaos is also fortunate, for it issues in creation. When Adam learns of redemption, he instinctively compares it to the creation.

> O goodness infinite, goodness immense!
> That all this good of evil shall produce
> And evil turn to good; more wonderful
> Than that which by creation first brought forth
> Light out of darkness!   (XII. 469–73)

Paradoxically, Milton's hostile chaos becomes a "good first matter" after all – but then, paradox is the pivot upon which the whole of Christian theology turns. Because chaos is evil, far from calling divine justice into account, it affirms it. Creation itself becomes the elegant means of frustrating Satan's ends, turning evil to good. When the angels in heaven rejoice over the creation, they sing

> Glory and praise, whose wisdom had ordain'd
> Good out of evil to create, instead
> Of Spirits malign a better Race to bring
> Into their vacant room, and thence diffuse
> His good to Worlds and Ages infinite.   (VII. 187–91)

Ultimately, Milton's use of the cosmogonic myth enables him to gather the full force of theodicy behind the simple words of Genesis: "and it was good."

With such a creation – a drama of salvation – Milton shifts his inquiry from the origin of evil to its end. He opens his epic imploring his muse to instruct him on the cause of evil.

> Say first, for Heav'n hides nothing from thy view
> Nor the deep Tract of Hell, say first what cause
> Mov'd our Grand Parents in that happy State,
> Favor'd of Heav'n so highly, to fall off...   (I. 27–30)

But in its deepest sense, that question is never answered in its own terms. Instead, Milton turns from the question to an assertion – of providence. The same pattern obtains in the Book of Job, where, of all of Milton's Biblical models, the theodical issue is most pressing. Job also begins asking why he suffers, and his question is "answered" in a very different key, with an assertion of divine omnipotence, and with what must have been especially striking for Milton, an assertion of Creation.

> Where were you when I laid the foundation of the earth?
> Tell me, if you have understanding.
> Who determined its measurements – surely you know!
> Or who stretched the line upon it?
> On what were its bases sunk, or who laid its cornerstone,
> when the morning stars sang together, and all the sons
> of God shouted for joy?　　　　　　　　　　(Job 38:4–7)

Yahweh goes on to describe the binding of evil, restraining of the waters of the deep, harnessing of Leviathan. It is this answer, the redemption from evil that a providential creation offers, that silences Job's fruitless inquiry into the origin of evil. That inquiry, we learned from the philosophers of hell, would have no end, in "wandring mazes lost." The singular appropriateness of Milton's audience for that first question "What cause?" now emerges, for Milton had asked the Muse of Creation.

> Instruct me, for Thou know'st; Thou from the first
> Wast present, and with mighty wings outspread
> Dove-like satst brooding on the vast Abyss
> And mad'st it pregnant:　　　　　　　　　　(I. 19–22)

Only one who made the abyss pregnant, who thereby redeemed chaos, can instruct Milton on the subject of evil, on its end in creation. Furthermore, it is Milton's own creation, an internal one that mirrors the cosmic *fiat lux* and raising of the firmament, that enables him to replace his question about divine justice with an assertion.

> 　　　　　　　　What in me is dark
> Illumine, what is low raise and support;
> That to the highth of this great Argument
> I may assert Eternal Providence
> And justify the ways of God to men.　　　　　(I. 22–26)

Woodhouse glances at a fascinating document of one of the ante-Nicene Fathers that sheds further light on Milton's chaos. In his dialogue, *Concerning Free-Will*, Methodius depicts a Valentinian explaining that originally matter:

"was without quality or form and, besides this, was borne about without order" ... that God did not leave it in this condition however, "but began to work upon it and wished to separate its best parts from its worst, and thus made all that was fitting for God to make out of it. But so much of it as was like lees, so to speak, this being unfitted for being made into anything, he left it as it was ... and from this ... what is evil has now streamed down among men."[58]

Now Milton is not a Valentinian, and he clearly associates evil with disobedience. Nonetheless, this separation of the lees and dregs at creation is reminiscent of a familiar Miltonic metaphor for the fall.

Good and evil we know in the field of this World grow up together almost inseparably; and the knowledge of good is so involv'd and interwoven with the knowledge of evill, and so many cunning resemblances hardly to be discern'd, that those confused seeds which were impos'd on *Psyche* as an incessant labor to cull out and sort asunder, were not more intermixt. It was from out the rinde of one apple tasted, that the knowledge of good and evill as two twins cleaving together leapt forth into the World. And perhaps this is that doom which Adam fell into of knowing good and evill, that is to say, of knowing good by evill.   (*Areopagitica*, 3. 514)

Milton "cannot praise a fugitive and cloistered virtue, unexercised and unbreathed, that never sallies out and sees her adversary" – not in man, and not in the universe. The crown of life is for him that endureth temptation (James 1:12), and just as the Son's righteousness is defined by his temptation, so, odd as it may sound, the Father's may be too. Chaos offers an awful temptation: not to create; to let darkness reign. And so, in Milton's scheme, creation, like all acts, becomes a choice – a choice, of course, that is freely made.

Once made, the choice to create out of chaos must be made again and again. The seventeenth century witnessed growing anxiety about the encroachment of chaos, detecting it in a general decay of nature. " 'Tis all in pieces, all coherence gone; / All just supply, and all relation" writes Donne in *An Anatomy of the World*. The notion that with man's fall all of nature was corrupted was an issue of public debate, with its main spokesman, Godfrey Goodman, offering the classic statement of the position in *The Fall of Man or the Corruption of Nature* (1616).[59] In 1627, George Hakewill published his attack against the prevailing idea of general corruption, *An Apology of the Power and Providence of God*, and Milton takes the same stand in an early academic exercise, *Naturam Non Pati Senium* (That Nature Is Not Subject to Old Age). In this paean to the eternal beauty, vigor, and order of the cosmos, Milton asserts that the stars do not swerve off their course and the planets are not slowing in their rotation.

37

At pater omnipotens fundatis fortius astris
Consuluit rerum summae, certoque peregit
Pondere fatorum lances, atque ordine summo
Singula perpetuum iussit servare tenorem.

$(33-36)^{60}$

That youthful confidence has sobered considerably by *Paradise Lost*. Here, the Anarch continually threatens, ready to reseize, or, rather, passively receive, the domain carved from him. The war in heaven is only the beginning, not the end, of the battle against Chaos. It is fought again at creation, at the fall, with Cain and Abel, at Babel and the flood; all of human history is played out on this battlefield. It will not be until the end of time, when the sea will be no more, that Chaos will retire forever, a broken foe.

One of his most devastating encroachments is given prominence of place in the last books of *Paradise Lost*: the flood. In *contrapasso* fashion, this punishment fits the crime; to destroy the reigning moral chaos, chaos is come again.

> but all the Cataracts
> Of Heav'n set open on the Earth shall pour
> Rain day and night, all fountains of the Deep
> Broke up, shall heave the Ocean to usurp
> Beyond all bounds, till inundation rise
> Above the highest Hills ....

(XI. 824–29)

The drama of creation is repeated. Mercy drives the waters of chaos back once more, and the dry ground appears just as "the good dry land" had done at the first creation. The "one just man" emerges from his ark/womb to a new world, and in his virtual birth-narrative he seconds the instinctive gesture of the first man at his birth, looking to heaven in gratitude. He who at the creation

> shut in the sea with doors,
> when it burst forth from the womb;
> when I made clouds its garment,
> and thick darkness its swaddling band,
> and prescribed bounds for it,
> and set bars and doors,
> and said, "Thus far shall you come, and no farther,
> and here shall your proud waves be stayed"

(Job 38:8–11)

now vows to defend his re-creation forever. Never again will the sea "surpass his bounds." And, in an echo of the perpetuity asserted at the end of *Naturam Non Pati Senium*, the Father promises that

Chaos vs. creation

> Day and Night,
> Seed-time and Harvest, Heat and hoary Frost
> Shall hold thir course, till fire purge all things new,
> Both Heav'n and Earth, wherein the just shall dwell.
> (XI. 898 – 901)

This divine initiative to keep chaos at bay must be answered with the corollary human choice against moral chaos. The Temptation is the beginning, not the end of that choice. Our final glimpse of Adam and Eve depicts them at the moment of decision – for chaos or creation.

> The World was all before them, where to choose
> Thir place of rest, and Providence thir guide:
> They hand in hand with wand'ring steps and slow
> Through Eden took thir solitary way. (XII. 646 – 49)

Among the many uses of the rich term ''wand'ring'' in the poem is an allusion to chaos: ''who shall tempt with wand'ring feet / The dark unbottom'd infinite Abyss'' (II. 404 – 05); and in its Latinate sense of erring, wandering suggests the moral chaos human history holds in store. But Adam and Eve also have the opportunity to choose a place of rest, a sabbath, the crown of creation. Milton's last picture captures them as they enter the fray, but he offers a hint of the triumph of creation, one made stronger by its former victories. The Son had left the gates of heaven to encounter the Abyss at creation just as they leave the gates of Paradise to behold the world all before them. And God has promised to ''raise another world,'' a new creation where man will find a place of rest, and perhaps in that paradise within, the sea will be no more.

2

"SECRET GAZE OR OPEN ADMIRATION": THE INVITATION TO ORIGINS

> The so-called drive for knowledge can be traced back to the drive to appropriate and conquer.   Nietzsche

Milton's preoccupation with chaos and creation is not restricted to the cosmic struggle. That drama is displaced onto the problem of knowledge of the creation, onto the expression of the creation, and onto another kind of creation, the poem. Furthermore, these categories continually blur: how to know becomes inseparable from how to speak of creation, and how to express the creation will become the heart of Milton's creative endeavor. In all of these displacements, chaos continually threatens. Access to the creation is difficult, if not impossible, for even seeking that knowledge is forbidden; and the question of whether Milton can express the creative light, "offspring of Heav'n first-born, / Or of th'Eternal Coeternal beam", *unblamed* is compounded when he is unsure of what it is he is expressing – with guilt or innocence.

In the course of Raphael's education of Adam, the angelic guide both incites and discourages his student's appetite for knowledge. Raphael does ultimately reveal the secrets of creation, "perhaps / Not lawful to reveal" (V. 569–70), but not without hedging his creation narrative round with lengthy discussions of illicit and licit knowledge. The subject of knowledge forms both the prologue and epilogue of the creation story proper. "Be lowly wise," the angel cautions an overly curious Adam, "Knowledge is as food, and needs no less / Her Temperance over Appetite" (VII. 126–27). Warnings about the limits of knowledge may reflect Milton's anxiety about the accessibility of creation; then again, they may even be a compensation for his failure to discover an origin. At any rate, Milton does not offer his account of creation with naive complacence about its authority; he worries about the legitimacy of the questions Adam asks and he worries about the status of the angel's answers, placing the inquiry into creation in an atmosphere tense with the possibility of violation.

Eventually, Milton will shift the very ground of that inquiry, from the accessibility of the object of knowledge to the posture of the seeker. Creation will become less an event "out there" to be discovered than the continual effort by a discoverer – creator. To be made in the Maker's image is to be a maker. The problem of knowledge has received much critical attention from Miltonists, and at the risk of rehearsing that discussion, I want to re-place it in another context. I would propose that the ground of the distinction between illicit and laudable knowledge is a deeper opposition, between invasive investigation and appreciation, and that this distinction deepens yet, into the more familiar one of chaos and creation. Knowledge born of a will to dominate an objectified creation "out there" leads to the return of chaos; knowledge which celebrates creations furthers the continual process of creation. This is why the battle between kinds of knowledge is waged in such proximity to the creation narratives; it is also why legitimate expressions of the creation – ones that are unblamed – are framed as a song of praise.

CURIOSITY AND KNOWLEDGE

Before he offers his account of creation, Raphael is enthusiastic about his student's hunger to know. Encouraging him, Raphael tells Adam not only that angels can partake of the human diet, but that man can aspire to share the angelic one. While he addresses Adam explicitly about food, "time may come when men / With Angels may participate and find / No inconvenient Diet" (V. 493 – 95), Adam is fully aware of the implicit analogy.

> O favorable Spirit, propitious guest,
> Well hast thou taught the way that might direct
> Our knowledge, and the scale of Nature set
> From centre to circumference, whereon
> In contemplation of created things
> By steps we may ascend to God.   (V. 507 – 12)

As the human diet is only the beginning of a cosmic system in which all is sustained and fed (culminating in the sun "supping" at evening with the ocean, imparting light to all and receiving "From all his alimental recompense" [V. 424]), so, too, human comprehension is only the beginning of the vast system of education, one that culminates in the revelation of the secrets of heaven itself. The thrust of Raphael's prologue to Adam's education, then, is that such an education is indeed possible. The bounties of earth may be compared to those of heaven (V. 432). Even as Raphael cautiously and elaborately delineates a theory of accommodation wherein our access to heavenly knowledge can only be approximate (at best), the angel doubles back – "though what if " – to suggest that heaven may not be categorically "other" after all.

> how shall I relate
> To human sense th'invisible exploits
> Of warring Spirits;
> ... how last unfold
> The secrets of another World, perhaps
> Not lawful to reveal? yet for thy good
> This is dispens't, and what surmounts the reach
> Of human sense, I shall delineate so,
> By lik'ning spiritual to corporal forms,
> As may express them best, *though what if* Earth
> Be but the shadow of Heav'n, and things therein
> Each to other like more than on Earth is thought?
> (V. 564–76, my emphasis)

Whether that shadow is interpreted Neoplatonically or typologically, the question ultimately bespeaks optimism in heavenward aspiration, an appropriate enough prelude to the angel's subsequent revelation of heavenly events.

But once the secrets are out, once Raphael begins to disclose knowledge of the heavens, he changes his note, as it were, to tragic. Heaven could not be farther: "Heav'n is for thee too high / To know what passes there" (VIII. 172–73); "so far, that earthly sight, / If it presume, might err in things too high, / And no advantage gain" (VIII. 120–22). The same analogy to food that once invited inquiry now stifles it, "Knowledge is as food, and needs no less / Her Temperance over Appetite" (VII. 126–27). Having encouraged Adam to inquire about creation, now Raphael tells him to "be lowly wise," and the angel tempers his own disclosure with like cautions: "to recount Almighty works / What words or tongue of Seraph can suffice, / Or heart of man suffice to comprehend?" (VII. 112–14). He is willing to answer Adam's desire for knowledge within bounds, but warns "beyond abstain / To ask" (VII. 120–21). While the notion of just boundaries is deeply imbedded in Milton's thought, this is an unexpected context for it. The enemy of licensing would hardly circumscribe knowledge. To cut off an inquiry would be to dismember truth, whose body must be restored instead. Milton addresses the issue of "subject matter" directly in *Areopagitica*. "They are not skilful considerers of human things who, imagine to remove sin by removing the matter of sin" (*CP*, 2, 527).

> Suppose we could expell sin by this means; look how much we thus expell of sin, so much we expell of vertue: for the matter of them both is the same; remove that, and ye remove them both alike. This justifies the high providence of God, who though he command us temperance, justice, continence, yet powrs out before us ev'n to a profusenes all desirable things, and gives us minds that can wander beyond all limit and satiety.
>
> (*CP*, 2, 527)

The contrary impulses that conclude this passage – insatiable thirst for knowledge "beyond all limit and satiety" but the need to temper that thirst – also inform Adam's education in *Paradise Lost*. The matter itself is neutral like the objects of knowledge; nonetheless, once again a discourse on knowledge has found its way into a discourse on sin.

What are we to make of the contradiction? Having revealed heaven's secrets – "not lawful to reveal" – is Raphael now retreating to the conventional piety of a retraction? Surely the impulse informing the medieval trope is antithetical to Milton. He would not want his writing discounted on the grounds that it is not scriptural, for he makes precisely the claim that it *is* scriptural; his Muse was the Muse of Moses, his testament the sequel to those other two. Hence he would not adopt either of the medieval solutions that distinguish a fictional text from the sacred one: Dante's or Chaucer's, allegory or denial.

Local explanations for Raphael's rebuke have been offered.[1] It seems that up until this point, Adam's curiosity is within bounds, but that now he has surpassed the limits of appropriate questions. Raphael is demonstrating precisely where the line must be drawn: at Adam's inquiry into planetary motion.

> When I behold this goodly Frame, this World
> Of Heav'n and Earth consisting, and compute
> Thir magnitudes, this Earth a spot, a grain,
> An Atom, with the Firmament compar'd
> And all her number'd Stars, that seem to roll
> Spaces incomprehensible (for such
> Thir distance argues and thir swift return
> Diurnal) merely to officiate light
> Round this opacous Earth, this punctual spot,
> One day and night; in all thir vast survey

Useless besides, reasoning I oft admire,
How Nature wise and frugal could commit
Such disproportions, with superfluous hand
So many nobler Bodies to create,   (VIII. 15–28)

Briefly, the problem that worries Adam is the economy of planetary movement. Can the earth, a mere "spot," warrant all of the motions of the sun, planet, and stars simply to produce day and night, "merely to officiate light"? Why should the other bodies, more numerous and "nobler" than our own, encircle the earth when it would be far more efficient for the earth to carry the burden of movement? The passage has spawned its own tradition of planetary speculation by students of Milton's astronomy.[2] But like the rest of Milton's astronomical observations, this dialogue is studiously designed to avoid taking up the cosmological controversy:[3] Satan flies from the outside shell of the world to the sun, "by centre or eccentric, *hard to tell*" (my emphasis). Instead, Adam presumably asks a forbidden question and Raphael silences it in order to teach a lesson in pragmatism. Raphael is delineating the proper limits of inquiry, and astronomy apparently violates those limits, for knowledge of the stars is of no immediate use to Adam. At least, this is Adam's interpretation of the injunction to "be lowly wise."

But apt the Mind or Fancy is to rove
Uncheckt, and of her roving is no end;
Till warn'd, or by experience taught, she learn
That not to know at large of things remote
From use, obscure and subtle, but to know
That which before us lies in daily life,
Is the prime Wisdom;   (VIII. 188–94)

This lesson in usefulness is what many have seized on as the definitive statement of Milton's view of learning, despite Milton's enthusiasm for a roving mind. I quote Lovejoy.

Thus the final conclusion which Milton expresses through his spokesmen in the dialogue – the thing, apparently, that he most wanted to say on the subject – is that these are matters about which it is useless and "impertinent," and even sinful for men to employ their minds. Milton's position, in short, is pragmatic, in the most vulgar sense of that ambiguous term, the sense in which it designated an obscurantist utilitarianism hostile to all disinterested intellectual curiosity and to all inquiry into unsolved problems about the physical world.[4]

These are strong words. It is doubtful that Milton could be hostile to learning, when he writes in *Of Education* that "The end then of learning is to repair the ruins of our first parents by regaining to know God aright, and out of that knowledge to love him''; hostile towards an investigation into the stars, when he writes in the *Seventh Prolusion* ''How much it means to grasp all the principles of the heavens and their stars, all the movements and disturbances of the atmosphere'';[5] hostile toward investigating the remote heavens, when he writes in the *Vacation Exercise* that with transported mind he would soar ''Above the Wheeling poles, and at heaven's door / Look in, and see each blissful Deity''. Then, too, the center of *Paradise Lost* is taken up with learning.

How, we might ask, does Raphael's disclosure of the creation, of the making of the sun and stars, the light and firmament, differ so markedly from the efforts of those whose ''quaint opinions'' about the cosmos provoke divine laughter? How are his musings about creation to be distinguished from those who ''come to model Heav'n / And calculate the Stars, how they will wield / The mighty frame, how build, unbuild'' the universe (VIII. 79 – 81)? And if the criterion for proper knowledge is usefulness, of what immediate use is the creation narrative to Adam? These are events that transpired long before his birth; they are certainly not ''That which before [him] lies in daily life'' (VIII. 193). Raphael does not, as well he might, caution Adam about the guise his enemy might appear in, or, say, about effective ways to balance mutual help with independence in order to prepare Adam for his argument with Eve about working apart. Compared to the kind of ''vulgar pragmatism'' Raphael might generously have offered, Adam's education does amount to so much ''fond impertinence.'' Viewed in this light, the dialogue about astronomy is tantamount to a dialogue about Milton's whole enterprise. ''For Milton, as for the encyclopedists, problems in natural philosophy reached their last solution only in divine philosophy.''[6] In other words, in Milton's universe, an inquiry into heavenly economy is no less than an inquiry into divine justice; to presume to question the *mechanical* workings of the universe is to presume to question the *theological* ones: both ask if the universe works right. If Adam asks the wrong questions – or too many questions, or presumptuous questions – then Milton does too. If there is something wasteful about the heavenly motions, is there not something essentially wasteful about the design of the moral life, wherein the full range of options is made available – a kind of profuseness within which man must define obedience? Given the outcome, is not Satan's freeing himself from hell, the fall of the rebel angels – the fall of man, for that matter – wasted motion? And perhaps there are one

too many trees in the Garden. Quaint opinions about the calcula-
tions of the stars, how to build and unbuild the universe, have large
implications for this poem.

Why does Milton's angel suggest that such inquiry is useless,
impertinent, even sinful, when the narrator proceeds to inquire into
the workings of the heavens himself? Why risk reducing *Paradise Lost*
to another "quaint opinion," or the butt of another divine joke?
Why would Milton have Raphael enjoin Adam to focus his attention
on what lies immediately before him, while he is intent on seeing
and telling of "things invisible to mortal sight"? Why does Milton
sabotage his theodicy in a dialogue on astronomy? There is another
way to ask questions about the stars. In another brief dialogue
on astronomy in *Paradise Lost* (IV. 657–88), Eve also questions
the economy of cosmic dispensation: is it not wasteful for the stars
to shine when no one beholds them? "But wherefore all night long
shine these, for whom / This glorious sight, when sleep hath shut
all eyes?" (IV. 657–58). Adam does not correct her for crossing the
bounds of permissible knowledge, nor does he caution her that an
inquiry into the heavens is beyond the scope of "low wisdom."
Instead, he tells her that the stars are posted in the heavens

> Lest total darkness should by Night regain
> Her old possession, and extinguish life
> In Nature and all things.
>
> (IV. 665–67)

The stars shine to keep chaos at bay. Furthermore, the stars inspire
a particular response which ultimately has this same order-affirming
effect. The stars

> though unbeheld in deep of night,
> Shine not in vain, nor think, though men were none,
> That Heav'n would want spectators, God want praise;
> Millions of spiritual Creatures walk the Earth
> Unseen, both when we wake, and when we sleep:
> All these with ceaseless praise his works behold
> Both day and night.
>
> (IV. 674–80)

Adam asserts that there is a proper way to approach the heavens
after all: to praise them. Nowhere in the later dialogue of Book VIII
does Raphael contradict this sentiment; in fact, he corroborates it.
Even as he conveys those cautions hostile to astronomical inquiry,
Raphael makes a subtle distinction.

> whether Heav'n move or Earth,
> Imports not, if thou reck'n right; the rest
> From Man or Angel the great Architect
> Did wisely to conceal, and not divulge
> His secrets *to be scann'd by them who ought*
> *Rather admire*;   (VIII. 70–75, my emphasis)

Presumably, the millions of unseen spirits who continually praise the creation do not simply *scan* the heavens, they *admire* them – heeding the root, they "wonder" or "marvel" at the heavens, a wonderment that finds expression in praise. If Adam's inquiry into the heavens issued in praise, it too would be permissible. Milton will say more on the subject yet. Praise is not simply a justification for presumptive curiosity, a palliative that takes the sting out of an essentially sinful drive to know. Praise is a worthy motive to inspire learning. As early as the *Seventh Prolusion*, entitled "Learning Makes Men Happier than Ignorance," Milton tells us, not that praise makes astronomical inquiries forgiveable, but that praise makes heavenly researches desirable – even necessary.

Scrutinize the face of all the world in whatever way you can. The Builder of this great work has made it for his own glory. The more deeply we search into its marvelous plan, into this vast structure with its magnificent variety – something which only Learning permits us to do – the more we honor its Creator with our admiration and follow him with our praise. In doing so we may be securely confident that we please Him.[7]

And "If learning is our leader and director in our quest for happiness, and if it has the approval of the Almighty and contributes to his praise, it surely cannot fail to make its followers happy in the very noblest way." Milton speaks of the purposefulness of learning again in *Of Education*, where the end of knowledge could not be more worthy: "The end of learning is to repair the ruins of our first parents by regaining to know God aright" (*CP*, 2, 366–67).

Even Satan is aware of this power of praise. Dissembling to Uriel, he pointedly interjects that piety underscores his "Unspeakable desire to see, and know / All these his wondrous works" (III. 662–63). When he claims that his motive is that "The Universal Maker we may praise" (III. 676), his disguise could not be more complete. This request for knowledge within the bounds of praise evokes an interesting answer from Uriel, one that sounds more like an appropriate response to Raphael than to Satan, for it is that other angelic commentator who speaks of excess and blame in knowledge-seeking.

47

Fair Angel, thy desire which tends to know
The works of God, thereby to glorify
The great Work-Master, leads to no excess
That reaches blame, but rather merits praise
The more it seems excess, that led thee hither
From thy Empyreal Mansion thus alone,
To witness with thine eyes what some perhaps
Contented with report hear only in Heav'n:
For wonderful indeed are all his works,
Pleasant to know, and worthiest to be all
Had in remembrance always with delight;

                                      (III. 694–704)

The Blakean exuberance of "the excess that merits praise the more
it seems excess" and the restraining impulse of "know to know no
more" again threaten to be irreconcilable; now it seems we must
choose between the authority of Uriel and Raphael. However,
Uriel's formula, that praise offers the simple resolution, is not so
simple nor so neat. He continues, beginning with a self-contradictory
"but," he doubles back:

But what created mind can comprehend
Thir number, or the wisdom infinite
That brought them forth, but hid thir causes deep.

                                      (III. 705–07)

The advocate of excess in knowledge stops short of pretending to
wisdom infinite: causes are hidden deep. Another turn follows. After
this last declaration of modesty, he plunges forth to recount the creation, a process not so incomprehensible to the created mind that it
prevents him from having witnessed it. If tradition recounts that man
was created last in order to bar him from the secrets of creation, Uriel
suffered no such exclusion.

I saw when at his Word the formless Mass,
This world's material mould, came to a heap:

                                      (III. 708–09)

The movement in this discourse parallels that of Adam's education
as a whole: advance (toward knowledge), retreat (from presumption), followed by disclosure of the hidden secret (the creation). And,
as in Adam's education, all of these steps are framed by an overarching purpose of praise: "the more / To magnify his works, the more we
know" (VII. 96–97). This movement is repeated, writ small, in
Adam's rehearsal of his own creation. Adam seems to understand
"low" wisdom as not pertaining to the cosmos but to his own

48

generation; that subject is the "lower flight" he descends to from the "high pitch" of his inquiry into the stars. But even with this intention to speak of things at hand, he disclaims, "For Man to tell how human Life began / Is hard; for who himself beginning knew?" (VIII. 250 – 51). He then proceeds to take up that hard task, beginning, significantly, with the narration of his first instinctive gesture heavenward – a gesture of praise – and concluding with the ceremonial praise of marriage. The creation is not only continually mediated – with Uriel's account to Satan, Raphael's to Adam, and Urania's to Milton – those accounts themselves are internally entangled with difficulty, marked, as they are, by oscillation between epistemological confidence and uncertainty.

These complex turns of thought about knowledge – advance, retreat, disclosure, with praise framing all – suggest that whatever praise is, it does not offer a simple resolution to a clear dichotomy. It does not negate the restraining impulse; rather praise subsumes the opposing categories to its larger purpose. A quest that is in the service of praise cannot aspire too high, cannot inquire too far. Presumption is not a quantitative category subject to objective measurement. Rather, presumption refers to a subjective intention. Praise can both incite the quest for knowledge and confer a natural limitation to the pursuit, for it converts mere learning – about the world – into wisdom, of things divine.[8]

This link between praise and knowledge is not unique to Milton. Standing behind his own reflections on the subject is the vast *curiositas* tradition.[9] The uses and abuses of knowledge preoccupied the ancients from Plato on. Classical definitions were repeated by the Fathers, among them, Seneca's "this desire to know more ... is a sort of intemperance"[10] and the Stoic "sapientia est rerum humanarum divinarumque scientia."[11] In the Renaissance, these were joined to the Psalter's "such things are too wonderful for me" and St. Paul's caveat, as rendered by George Wither:

> Above thy knowledge do not rise,
> But, with sobriety, be wise.[12]

My purpose is not to survey the *curiositas* tradition here. The story of the development of theories on the origin and end of knowledge constitutes the history of philosophy, science, and even religion.[13] Such histories have been written. I do, however, want to take up one of its central figures for the light he sheds on Milton.

Augustine's influence is both direct – Milton alludes to his works explicitly throughout his prose – and indirect.[14] In a breathless summary of the theologian's contribution, Howard Schultz indicts him for lapsing into exactly the kinds of contradictions we have noted in Milton.

Augustine had transmitted to an unbroken line of medieval disciples, to Christian skeptics of the Renaissance, and to all Protestantism, a volume of precept that hardly fitted his own practice; for it was he who originated or popularized most of the speculations that Renaissance critics like to saddle upon Scholasticism.... He played with bizarre analogies in his defense of the Trinity, with theories of the soul's origin in his work on free will and foreknowledge, with natural science in his comment on the letter of Genesis; and whether answers came to him or escaped him ... he littered his pages with lectures to admonish the curious. His commentary on Genesis had raised too many unanswered questions, he owned in his retractions (ii, 1). No theory of the soul's origins seriously mattered, he once remarked while wading through all the theories.[15]

Nonetheless, in the *Confessions* Augustine's primary interest, like Milton's, is in the function of knowledge: not the objects sought, but the religious posture of the seeker. Even though star-gazing was the exemplum of sinful curiosity – the image of Thales gazing fixedly at the stars as he falls into a well was familiar in emblem books – Augustine does not take issue with the astronomers because they inquire into the heavens, nor does he reject scientific pursuits per se. To the contrary, he prefers the findings of the ''secular scientists'' to those of the Manicheans because they are empirically verifiable. His objection to the astronomers is that they research the heavens for the wrong reason; they seek knowledge for its own sake, without reference to the Creator. As Hans Blumenberg summarizes,

Augustine connects the mistake that he sees in *curiositas* neither with a particular object, such as the astronomical one, nor with authentically theoretical insistence on precision and verifiability but only with unreflectiveness in the use of reason, which as such already constitutes denial of the debt of gratitude for being created.[16]

In Augustine's words, the astronomers

lapse into pride without respect for you, my God, and fall into shadow away from your light, but although they can predict an eclipse of the sun so far ahead, they can not see that they themselves are already in the shadow of eclipse. This is because they ignore you and do not inquire how they came to possess the intelligence to make these researches.[17]

Astronomical speculation lapses into the sin of curiosity when it lacks the motive of gratitude. Augustine turns the stars to his own literary end to make the point.

They [Manichaean astronomers] do not know this way, but think themselves as high and as bright as the stars; and this is why they have fallen to earth and their *senseless hearts grow benighted*. Much of what they say about the created world is true, but they do not search with piety for the Truth, its Creator. This is why they do not find him; or, if they do find him and *have the knowledge of God, they do not honour him or give thanks to him as God.*[18]

This is no discussion of "mere" astronomy either. The light/shade, bright/benighted inversions above typify Biblical descriptions of the moral life. They are also a familiar Miltonic device.

> He that has light with in his own clear breast
> May sit i'th' center, and enjoy bright day,
> But he that hides a dark soul and foul thoughts
> Benighted walks under the midday Sun;
> Himself is his own dungeon.
>
> (*Comus*, 381–85)

Only a reference to blindness is needed to complete the Miltonic formula. Augustine does not disappoint: the astronomers "attribute to themselves what is yours, and in the same perverse blindness they try to ascribe their own qualities to you."[19] Milton plays at length with the notion of interior light and external darkness in the *Second Defense*, claiming to prefer his blindness to that of his enemies, for "in proportion as I am blind, I shall more clearly see."[20] Both speak, of course, of blindness to the Maker, one induced by a rigid focus on the objects of the world.

All of the vices Augustine links to curiosity emerge in Satan's quest for knowledge: lust, the appetite for information; avarice, the mastery over objects of the world gained by such information; and pride, the elevation of the self as possessor of once hidden secrets. In the absence of a purposeful quest for the Maker, knowledge-seeking ultimately redounds upon a promotion of the self.[21]

Just as no one can exist of himself, so neither can anyone be wise of himself, but only by the enlightening influence of Him of whom it is written, "All wisdom cometh from the Lord."

(*Enchiridion*, 1, 1–3)

Augustine personalizes the dire consequences of an inquiry that is not grounded in praise:

I used to talk glibly as though I knew the meaning of it all, but unless I had looked for the way which leads to you in Christ our Saviour, instead of finding knowledge I should have found my end.[22]

To be devoted to the self is to be, like Satan, "to Death devote." Such Satanic knowledge *is* forbidden knowledge.

Raphael's injunction to Adam to limit his vision to the immediate, to that which concerns him, takes on new meaning in this Augustinian context. Usefulness need no longer be defined with recourse to either Irene Samuel's qualification – what is useful in the Garden – or Lovejoy's restriction of the term's meaning to "vulgar pragmatism." Nothing could be more useful to Adam than that which directs him to his Maker, inspiring praise. The world is useful, Augustine tells us, as an instrument of salvation, so long as the instrument is not mistaken for the goal.[23] He offers images of entanglement and entrapment to describe fascination with the immediate world: a lizard catching flies, a spider entangling them in her web.[24] Such curiosity is a temptation meant to divert us from that noble end of learning, "to know God aright." Augustine refers to it as the lust of the eye. "For all that is in the world, the lust of the flesh and the lust of the eyes and the pride of life, is not of the Father but is of the world" (1 John 2:16).[25] In these terms, the peril of curiosity is to be myopic, rather than to look too far. What is nearest at hand and what is humanly remote become inverted, for "what is nearest at hand is the perception and acknowledgment of the dependence of one's own capacity for truth upon illumination."[26] That is, what is most useful is acknowledgment of contingency, for it is the ground of gratitude. This is the "low wisdom" of Job: "Behold, the fear of the Lord, that is wisdom, and to depart from evil is understanding" (28:28, AV). In this sense, the stars may well be of *immediate* concern to Adam.

Usefulness must be determined by the motive for study, and not the object studied. To make that point, Augustine dissociates sinful curiosity from the image of the stars by speaking of them in two opposing senses. To look again at his passage on the misguided approach of the astronomers:

They do not know this way, but think themselves as high and as bright as the stars; and this is why they have fallen to earth and *their senseless hearts grow benighted*.[27]

That sentence contains part of the plot of *Paradise Lost*: Lucifer is the morning star who falls for presumption. But I have truncated Augustine's discussion; he continues, explaining that the quest for the stars need not be presumptuous:

Yet these men do not know that he [Christ] is the way by which they must come down from the heights where they have set themselves and rise again, with him, to be with him.

According to tradition, Christ is also a star; having died as the evening star, he is resurrected as the star of the morning. Thus, Augustine completes the sacred history depicted in *Paradise Lost*: there is a proper path to aspire heavenward.

THINGS VISIBLE TO MORTAL SIGHT

Milton explores both motives for knowledge, seeking to distinguish the knowledge that is presumptive from that which aspires lawfully. In *Paradise Lost*, that distinction in motives becomes especially sharp with reference to knowledge of the creation, how to "build, unbuild" the universe. Over against the millions of unseen spirits who praise the creation are the fallen angels who first hear of creation as a rumor. Having denied the Maker, they can have only uncertain knowledge of his making. In fact, it is as rumor that the first mention of the creation in *Paradise Lost* is made, and it arises in the context of the debate in hell, far afield from even the mediated eye-witness accounts of Uriel and Raphael. In hell, creation is not the subject of an education in gratitude; it is offered as the solution to the infernal demand for revenge. Casting about for an "easier enterprise" than the invasion of heaven, Beelzebub proposes the invasion of this new realm.

> There is a place
> (If ancient and prophetic fame in Heav'n
> Err not) another World, the happy seat
> Of some new Race call'd *Man*, about this time
> To be created like to us, though less
> In power and excellence, but favor'd more
> Of him who rules above;   (II. 345–51)

Infernal curiosity is born. The alternative to that noble end of learning, "to know God aright," is "To waste his whole Creation" (II. 365).

> Thither let us bend all our thoughts, to learn
> What creatures there inhabit, of what mould,
> Or substance, how endu'd, and what thir Power,
> And where thir weakness, how attempted best,
> By force or subtlety: (II. 354–58)

To search out the land, to conquer and invade it, to repopulate it with the new inhabitants of Sin and Death: the paradigm for Satanic knowledge is knowledge as reconnaissance.[28] In this reconnaissance mode, the object of knowledge is seen as the enemy. Research becomes an assessment of weakness to prey upon. Discovery is of the most effective way to entice the enemy into his own destruction: how to "attempt" man best, "By force or subtlety." Here, the double sense of "attempt" – "to assay" and "to tempt" – links investigation to undoing. Knowledge of the creation is sought, not to praise it, but to gain control over it, to seize and ultimately to destroy it. As Satan explains to Sin, he goes on the "uncouth errand" of confirming the rumor of creation in order to destroy it.

> Be this or aught
> Than this more secret now design'd, I haste
> To know, and this once known, shall soon return,
> And bring ye to the place where Thou and Death
> Shall dwell at ease,   (II. 837–41)

The predatory character of that research is epitomized by Satan's approach to Paradise.

> As when a prowling Wolf,
> Whom hunger drives to seek new haunt for prey,
> Watching where Shepherds pen thir Flocks at eve.
>   (IV. 183–85)

Such knowledge is not given; it is stolen – "as a Thief bent to unhoard the cash / Of some rich Burgher" (IV. 188–89) – and the sense of violating, or raping, evokes the project of Mammon, who "Ransack'd the Center, and with impious hands / Rifl'd the bowels of thir mother Earth / For Treasures better hid" (I. 686–88). If praise suggests appreciation and respect for the autonomy of the object, Satanic knowledge is aggressive – the object must be acted upon – and mastering: the devils intend to "possess / All as our own" (II. 365–66). Thus Satan forgoes his initial involuntary gaze of appreciation for the more active survey of his prey. Milton joins Augustine in associating knowledge with sight – curiosity was the lust of the *eye* – and both anticipate much later psychoanalytic discussions of knowledge-seeking as a form of scopophilia. Milton's key figure for one who seeks knowledge in order to master the object of inquiry is the voyeur. Freud couples scopophilia (voyeurism) with sadism as impulses of aggression against an object; the voyeur is no innocent on-looker; rather, he looks in order to gain mastery over the object of his sight. To *spy* upon creation is to be its enemy. Raphael did not witness Adam's birth because that day he was guarding the gates of hell

> To see that none thence issu'd forth a spy,
> Or enemy, while God was in his work,

The invitation to origins

Lest hee incenst at such eruption bold,
Destruction with Creation might have mixt.
(VIII. 233–36)

Just spying on creation would provoke its destruction. The impulse to seize control is also apparent in the voyeuristic gaze of Satan who watches Paradise from a position of concealment, seeing, but unseen. When he perches himself upon the tree of life as a cormorant, we learn that he "only us'd / For prospect, what well us'd had been the pledge / Of immortality" (IV. 199–201); that "prospect" is offered as the antithesis of eternal life because the eye of Satan is lethal. Satan will inhabit more predatory creatures, looking and learning to gain mastery, "unespied / To mark what of thir state he more might learn / By word or action markt" (IV. 399–401). His sightings are not so much a prelude to attacking his prey, as they are the first phase of the attack: his eye is his weapon.

> about them round
> A Lion now he stalks with fiery glare,
> Then as a Tiger, who by chance hath spi'd
> In some Purlieu two gentle Fawns at play,
> Straight couches close, then rising changes oft
> His couchant watch, as one who chose his ground
> Whence rushing he might surest seize them both
> Gript in each paw: (IV. 401–08)

Adam and Eve are not the sole victims of his sight; he resolves that "with narrow search I must walk round / This Garden, and no corner leave unspi'd" (IV. 528–29), making those rounds with "sly circumspection."

In "Instincts and Their Vicissitudes" (1915), Freud outlines a mechanism of reversal in which the aggression toward an object is turned back upon the self, and the once active subject (sadist, voyeur) assumes the role of passive object (masochist, exhibitionist).[29] Because in "normal" seeing, the roles of object and subject are continually substituted, either of the extremes – only seeing or only showing – represent a hysterical fixation.[30] That response is driven by the fear of loss. In order to shift positions, the scopophiliac must move his gaze away from the object and endure temporary loss until he can become the object of another's sight. Similarly, the exhibitionist will not vacate his object position for fear that it will be left empty. When Satan is apprehended by Uriel, the dreaded event occurs: the viewer is viewed. Tellingly, Satan is far more preoccupied about loss than about having his destructive scheme spoiled.

Know ye not then said *Satan*, fill'd with scorn,
Know ye not mee? ye knew me once no mate
For you, there sitting where ye durst not soar;
Not to know mee argues yourselves unknown,

(IV. 827 – 30)

Again, to be rigidly entrenched in either the subject or object position is to avoid the other role; the voyeur hides and the exhibitionist does not see.

Has the narrator made his blindness a figure for the unseeing exhibitionist? If he could see, he may only encounter a universal blank beyond the universal blank of his darkness; there may be no sight of God, there may be no justification of God's ways. And so he wards off that fear by displaying himself. The blind narrator conquers object loss by making himself an object of sight. He conjures a presence that is all-seeing – "Heav'n hides nothing from the view" (I. 27) – he requests a "fit audience" (VII. 31), and he nakedly displays his own ambition to his readers (IX. 13 – 19, 25 – 45). He revisits a lamp that may illuminate him, but does not enable him to see – "thou / Revist'st not these eyes, that roll in vain / To find thy piercing ray, and find no dawn" (III. 22 – 24). Others have concluded that a writer's initial scopophilia, his observation of both real and imaginary lives, turns into exhibitionism at the process of composition when he displays his sights to others.[31] But the maneuver of the narrator of *Paradise Lost* is more complicated still. The process of his disclosure recapitulates the movements that characterized disclosure of the creation and Adam's birth narrative: advance (he confidently sees); retreat (he turns his gaze away, apologetically and guiltily, almost as if he had been apprehended); and then, and only then, full disclosure. Those stages describe even the first few lines of the invocation to light. In the first line, the narrator confidently sees the light: "Hail holy Light, offspring of Heav'n first-born." In the second, he turns away (hinting of guilty seeing), to exhibit himself: "May I express thee unblam'd?" And then he proceeds to the full disclosure: "since God is Light, / And never but in unapproached Light / Dwelt from Eternity, dwelt then in thee, / Bright effluence of bright essence increate" (III. 3 – 6). This pattern of advance, retreat, followed by disclosure, is repeated throughout an invocation that resists conforming readily to either extreme category, exhibitionism or scopophilia. Instead, it thematizes and works through guilty looking and blind showing, alternating between the two and finally transcending those options.[32] The narrator reascends from the Stygian darkness to light; he still cannot see and becomes the object of sight; but then he visits the Muses' haunts: "Yet not the more / Cease I to wander" (III. 26 – 27). In that final position, he looks – not from a position of concealment – but openly, showing even as he sees.

If the voyeur *willingly* assumes the position of object momentarily, fretting that he cannot see accurately (as Raphael does) or complaining that he cannot see at all (as the narrator does), then he cannot be caught in the act of looking. He cannot be made a guilty object involuntarily. But as he looks, he risks imitating the vision of Satan, the mastering destructive curiosity that Adam is cautioned against, Satan is punished for, and Eve experiences in her dream of "high exaltation" to "a prospect wide." How is the narrator's sight any less culpable than Satan's, how can he see and tell of things invisible to mortal sight, *unblamed*?

Giving up seeing to become an object of sight entitles him to see again, this time, to see and *tell*. Milton's strategy is to distinguish between "secret gaze" and "open admiration." When Satan asks Uriel for directions to the new world, we know that he is on a mission of destruction even as he protests that his motive is to praise the universal Maker. He claims to seek man so that "with secret gaze, / Or open admiration him behold" (III. 671 – 72). The lie is oddly predictive since his response to the sight of man is mixed, reversing, as he does, from open adoration to secret gaze. But the distinction between the two ways of looking, the two ways of knowing, is so apparent to the reader that it can serve as a source of dramatic irony. Open admiration escapes either of the hysterical responses of voyeurism (in which one is entrenched as the seeing subject who cannot be seen) and exhibitionism (in which one maintains the position of the object of sight, avoiding becoming the seeing subject). The subject who admires *openly* is willing to be simultaneously the subject and the object of sight rather than rigidly adhere to one position or the other. He sees, admiringly, and he is seen, openly. By telling, he emerges from the voyeur's position of concealment. This is the position Milton's narrator ultimately aspires to when he both sees and shows, to "see and tell / Of things invisible to mortal sight" (III. 54 – 55).

For all of his self-concealment, the Father also escapes occupying the position of voyeur fixedly. If the "invisible King ... hath supprest in Night" his hidden secrets not to be scanned, he has also expressed those secrets, shown himself, in creation, where, like the narrator, he writes them in the "book of knowledge fair." Furthermore, while the watching Father is concealed behind skirts "Dark with excessive bright" (even the seraphim must veil their eyes), he has expressed the "effulgence of his Glory" in his visible Son, "In whose conspicuous countenance, without cloud / Made visible, th' Almighty Father shines" (III. 380, 388, 385–86).[33] Rigid adherence to the position of voyeur or exhibitionist presents another threat of chaos. When Adam and Eve attempt to peer into heaven, they fall, ushering in the return of chaos. To look openly, as seeing subject and as object who shows, is to imitate divine seeing, expressing the creation, and thereby sustaining it. Secrets should not be scanned but admired. Even when Milton early announced his intention to "at Heav'n's door / Look in, and see each blissful Deity," he accompanied that ambition to see with the ambition to show: "I have some naked thought that rove about / And loudly knock to have their passage out."[34]

"Secret gaze, / *Or* open admiration": that use of the Miltonic "or" is symptomatic of a larger point. This distinction, between seeing and knowing in order to devour, and seeing and knowing in order to praise, can have no resolution. By leaving the dichotomy between them gaping wide, Milton forces a choice. When Adam first asks Raphael to tell him the story of creation, he acknowledges that distinction and is very careful to ally himself explicitly with one purpose over against the other.

> what cause
> Mov'd the Creator in his holy Rest
> Through all Eternity so late to build
> In *Chaos* ...
>   if unforbid thou mayst unfold
> What wee, *not to explore the secrets ask*
> *Of his Eternal Empire, but the more*
> *To magnify his works, the more we know.*
> (VII. 90–97, my emphasis)

In *Paradise Regained*, Satan offers Christ knowledge from a prospect view – the predatory, imperialistic variety.

> Be famous then
> By wisdom; as thy Empire must extend,
> So let extend thy mind o'er all the world,
> In knowledge, all things in it comprehend.
> (IV. 221–24)

But to his offer of Greek learning, Christ responds that they have nothing to teach, "Ignorant of themselves, of God much more, / And how the world began" (IV. 310–11); that is, he responds with an expression of even his own contingency.

Clearly, Milton does not make light of the temptation: one is Christ-like to respond so. This most learned of poets neither glosses over the possibility of curiosity being sinful, nor does he buffer the consequences. To seek forbidden knowledge by forbidden means is, as Adam confesses in Book XII, to fall. Furthermore, Milton has not distanced himself from the problem, objectifying voyeurism into only an approach Satan might take or an option Adam must confront. In that most personal of poetic occasions, the invocation, Milton faces the problem head-on, expressing the apprehension that his own inquiries may be forbidden, that his own revelations may be only quaint conjectures, and that his own aspirations may be, after all, presumptions – punishable by blindness. He offers the figure of Bellerophon who, for his heavenward research, falls on the alien field to wander in blindness and loneliness until his death.

Overtly, what distinguishes Milton from Bellerophon – and it is the distinction between wisdom and curiosity – is the invocation itself. The dependence upon his Muse is an acknowledgment of contingency, and the very expression of that contingency redeems him from guilty seeing. But Milton is more subtle yet. In his final comment on the dialogue on astronomy, Milton turns the forbidden stars – the remote heavens that could have been a snare – into an invitation, indeed, into his very Guide. For in the only reference to the proper name of his Muse in the poem, Milton identifies her as Urania – the Muse of Astronomy. When Milton appropriates the goddess of the stars, he associates her with the allegorical Wisdom of Proverbs, making them both witness to the creation. And having witnessed creation, Urania, and Wisdom, her sister, are qualified to offer knowledge, not rumor or quaint opinions of it.

> Instruct me, for Thou know'st; Thou from the first
> Wast present   (I. 19–20)

Milton thereby converts star-gazing, the emblem of presumptive curiosity, into a divinely sanctioned quest – into, that is, revelation. Milton's Thales does not fall into the well; he sees and tells of things invisible to mortal sight.

3

"REMEMBER AND TELL OVER": CREATION IN SACRED SONG

If a word which I use is to have meaning I must "commit myself"
by its use. If you commit yourself, there are consequences.

Wittgenstein

I turn now to Milton's other creation, the poem, and its relation to
chaos, that void wherein he "poises his fictive world" much as his
"pendant world" is poised in the abyss. I do not impose that analogy;
it is Milton who explicitly compares his poetic creation to the birth
of the cosmos at the outset of his poem. Milton implores the Creator-
deity, who "Dove-like satst brooding on the vast Abyss / And mad'st
it pregnant" (*PL* I. 21–22, Gen. 1:2), who decreed the light and
raised the waters from the deep, similarly to empower him.

> What in me is dark
> Illumine, what is low raise and support;
>
> (I. 22–23)

If Milton's poetic universe is *created* like the universe, it is also
threatened like it. *Fiat lux* is meant to be understood as a performative
utterance – the ideal enactment with words – and to encounter
the threat that the light may fail, that the raised firmament may
collapse back into chaos, as Milton does, is ultimately to fear for
language, to fear, that is, for the power of language to act effectively.
Milton does worry about whether *Paradise Lost* works. The figure of
the overly curious Bellerophon is invoked in close proximity to
Orpheus, and the fates of the presumptuous knowledge-seeker and
the ineffective singer are versions of the same failure: one is blinded
and the other unheard. Seeing is not the only difficulty Milton
depicts; showing – that is, singing – is attended by its own dangers.
If an ongoing battle between chaos and creation describes Milton's
subject, it also continually informs his process.

60

Creation in sacred song

To say that Milton's creation is imperilled even as he describes it is not to say enough; it is *especially* when Milton thematizes creation, both the divine cosmic one and his own, that the danger is most acute. That same anxiety gives rise to dialogues in which Raphael hedges over the status of his creation narrative and invocations in which the narrator is preoccupied with the status of his poetic creation. It has often been noted that in the invocation to Book I, even when Milton first boasts that his effort is "unattempted yet in Prose or Rhyme," he also makes the dark side of that boast explicit: only twenty-eight lines later, he speaks of another "attempt" and it, he tells us, is vain. He barely concludes the description of his ambition to soar with "no middle flight" when he speaks of another soaring ambition: the effort of one who aspires "To set himself in Glory above his peers." He invokes the aid of his Muse for his "adventurous song," but adventure has decidedly presumptuous connotations: Eve's fall marks her as "adventrous" (IX. 921) and Satan's effort to destroy the new world is his "adventure" (X. 468).[1] By the time Milton addresses the light in the invocation to Book III – "may I express thee unblam'd?" – he has already raised the specter of blame persistently and dramatically enough to make us wonder how expression can be blameless.

Nor is the pattern one of diminishing anxiety as his own expression gathers momentum. If, in the invocation to Book III, the complex interplay of allusions to sight and blindness convey moments of despair that are finally eclipsed by supreme confidence – "So much the rather thou Celestial Light / Shine inward" (III. 51 – 52) – that confidence in his poetic endeavor dims by the invocation to Book VII. Here the narrator offers vivid images of the failure of imaginative order and the danger awaiting poetic ambition, depicting a savage clamor that drowns the voice of the poet as the "noises loud and ruinous" of chaos threaten to drown the Creating Word. With this invocation forming the prologue to Raphael's narrative of the cosmic creation, the narrator also has managed to make his own chaos the prelude to that other creation.

> But drive far off the barbarous dissonance
> Of *Bacchus* and his Revellers, the Race
> Of what wild Rout that tore the *Thracian* Bard
> In *Rhodope*, where Woods and Rocks had Ears
> To rapture, till the savage clamor drown'd
> Both Harp and Voice; nor could the Muse defend
> Her Son.   (VII. 32 – 38)

With the prospect of completion now before him – "Half yet remains unsung" (VII. 21) – his most horrific image of its failure surfaces: the wild rout with their dissonant clamor will leave his half-yet-remaining song unsung forever. Milton seems to be pausing midway in his narration, like Michael does at the flood, between one world created and the fear of one destroyed. If he is "more safe" in one sense, he is "with dangers compast round" in another. Nonetheless, he will create, not only *with* this constant threat to his own ambition, but also *from* it, constructing an apparatus to defend himself from the fate of the undefended Orpheus. His words must not be ineffective, must not be silenced by the dissonant roar; his epic must not be left to the impotent defense of the epic Muse who forsook Orpheus. Milton's epic must do more than epics do: his voice must hold in rapture, not just rocks and woods, but the threatening clamor of chaos itself.

Even while the invocations express the encroachment of chaos, they also embody the will to dispel it: to call upon, *invocare*, is to anticipate an answer. In his discussion of apostrophe, Jonathan Culler notes that invoking a presence also betrays an absence, more specifically, a discomfort with that absence that the apostrophe functions to "fill in." But the addressee is not the presence conjured by apostrophe; rather, it is the presence of the poet, who is constituted by virtue of his expectation of receiving an answer. "The object is treated as a subject, an *I* which implies a certain type of *you* in its turn."[2] Milton would add a moral valence to this formulation. Had Orpheus called upon the heavenly rather than the profane Muse, his voice would not have been drowned, for to call upon a heavenly Muse is to assume the position of worshipper. If romantic poets adopt the voice of the visionary, addressing nature because they expect an answer from her, Milton assumes the voice of the redeemed, of one whose prayers are heard. Culler makes the observation that in our embarrassment over apostrophe, we reduce the vocative to description, "eliminating that which attempts to be an event." What is at stake in apostrophe is what is at stake in Milton's enterprise: "the power of poetry to make something happen."[3]

That power is not self-evident; again, if the invocation conjures a presence, it also betrays an absence. In his first invocation, Milton commands his Muse to "instruct" him, "for thou knowst"; he would become, thereby, an authorized pupil. But calling upon her also acknowledges his fear that no one is there to hear, his isolation and his lack of authorization: "this figure which seems to establish relations between the self and the other can in fact be read as an act of radical interiorization and solipsism.''[4] In the last invocation, he does not address the Muse directly, and he doubts the authenticity of the heavenly voice. The utterance that had once been an active call is now only descriptive, an uneasy description at that: "*if* all be mine, / Not Hers" (IX. 46–47, my emphasis). Given the narrator's dependence on the authenticating power of calling, answering, and answerability, even to doubt his Muse is to raise the specter of a failed project again. And that poetic chaos is, once again, bound to the universal one: "if all be *his*," then nature may be subject to old age and the return of chaos after all (IX. 44–47).

Contrary to Dr. Johnson's sense of the invocations as ''short digressions'' that ''might doubtless be spared,'' they are not isolated instances of the impulse to call upon. Throughout *Paradise Lost*, in order to express divinity unblamed, Milton would express it as prayer. From his Biblical models, he has selected one kind of hymn, not a cry for deliverance, not – even in a poem about loss – a lamentation, but a song of praise. Invocations are not only epic markers, they are also the determining feature of a hymn of praise.[5] *Paradise Lost* is punctuated by such songs – the aubade of Adam and Eve, the nightly song of millions of unseen spirits, and the hymns of the angelic hosts at the creation – but I want to make a larger claim, that *Paradise Lost* itself strives to constitute such a sacred song. This epic would not just describe, but enact; not just depict praise, but praise. Malinowski wrote that ''perhaps nothing demonstrates more clearly that words are acts and that they function as acts than the study of sacred utterances.''[6] What may be unattempted yet in prose or rhyme is virtually a sacred utterance, a hymn of praise, in the form of a classical epic. When Milton complains about the inferior ''argument'' of the epic tradition, we know that he still does not leave war and love behind; the wrath of Achilles becomes a type for divine wrath and Lavinia ''disespous'd'' a type for Eve. Instead, the failure of those epics may be, for Milton, their failure to achieve a style answerable to a celestial patroness, the failure of language to perform and to provoke her response.[7]

In thus empowering words, Milton heeds the Bible even as he anticipates contemporary debates about the illocutionary force of language.[8] Deuteronomy tells us that ''If the word does not come to pass and is not true, the thing does not take place or come true'' (18:22, my translation). In Hebrew, the term for word and act is the same: *dabar*. Imitating the Priestly writer's account of creation by word, Milton's account has the Father tell the Son ''how to do things with words'' in the grand style: ''speak thou, and be it done''

(VII. 164). And while his golden compasses may sketch the circumference of the cosmos, those bounds are only established upon declaration: "Thus far extend, thus far thy bounds, / This be thy just Circumference, O World" (VII. 230–31). In the psalms, calls are not descriptive; they are cast as events, meant to invite the further event of a response. "Hear, O Lord, when I cry aloud" (Ps. 27:7); "Praise is due to thee, O God, in Zion, and to thee shall vows be performed, O thou who hearest prayer" (Ps. 65:1). The belief that the act of the utterance is understood to inspire further acts governs not only the psalms but the narrative of ancient Israel itself.

And the Lord said, I ... have heard their cry by reason of their taskmasters; for I know their sorrows; and I am come down to deliver them out of the hands of the Egyptians, (Ex. 3:7,8, AV)

Reformers were well aware of this Biblical sense of the power of language.[9] Luther wrote, "Opera Dei sunt verba eius ... idem est facere et dicere Dei" (God's works are his words ... his doing is identical with his speaking).[10] With words the primary weapon in the Puritan revolt, variations on Revelation 19:15 abounded: "From his mouth issues a sharp sword." John Preston implored God to make the word

lively and mighty in operation, to cut down your lusts, to pierce as a two-edged sword, dividing betweene the bones and the marrow, the joynts and the spirit; that is, that you may know your selves better than you did before.[11]

The Bible's words were not only an effective sword; they also fed and healed according to the preface to the Geneva Bible.

Nonethelesss, the perils attending such an understanding of language did not escape Milton. The command not to eat the fruit of the forbidden tree in the Garden does not have the same force that the word of God has in the prophecy of Amos, where that word lights on Mt. Carmel and it withers (Amos 1:2). Austin acknowledges that frequently the conditions for successful performance are imperfect (infelicitous), but he still sees this risk as a deviation from a norm when the "right" conventions are attached to speech-acts. Derrida has argued that the "risks" which attend performatives are not separable from them, for the risk is interpretation itself, "with all its hazards and uncertainties."[12] According to Derrida, the difficulty attending the performative utterance is the same as that awaiting any utterance, the murky realm of interpretation. That "perdition" invades all language, as chaos does order.

does the quality of risk admitted by Austin *surround* language like a kind of *ditch* or external place of perdition which speech could never hope to leave, but which it can escape by remaining at "home?" ... Or, on the contrary, is this risk rather its internal and positive condition of possibility? Is that outside its inside, the very force and law of its emergence?[13]

No one demonstrates the power of this argument better than Satan in *Paradise Lost*. He intercepts an utterance fully designed to be effective: the command not to eat the fruit of the tree of knowledge. Between utterance and reception, Satan infuses the problematics of interpretation.[14] He asks who said it, with what intention, under what circumstances, how could the author really mean to prohibit, and what did he *really* mean. Definitions are unstable: disobedience turns into a "petty trespass" and then heroism in the face of death, but then, what does *death* mean? His barrage of questions releases the uncertainties of interpretation with a vengeance, ultimately rendering the command powerless.

> will God incense his ire
> For such a petty Trespass, and not praise
> Rather your dauntless virtue, whom the pain
> Of Death denounc't, whatever thing Death be,
> Deterr'd not from achieving what might lead
> To happier life, knowledge of Good and Evil;
> Of good, how just? of evil, if what is evil
> Be real, why not known, since easier shunn'd?
>
> (IX. 692–99)

Milton will explore the failure of language to perform elsewhere: there are insincere songs, song that "charm the Sense" (II. 556). False praise is the dominant mode of temptation in *Paradise Lost* as well as in *Comus* and in *Samson Agonistes*. Misplaced praise is one of the consequences of the fall: Eve immediately praises the tree. For all of Milton's effort to depict that most effective prayer of the repentant Adam and Eve and to infuse his own epic with prayer, he also offers, in Satan's soliloquy, an example of a prayer that does not work. Satan's invocation perverts the convention – "to thee I call / But with no friendly voice, and add thy name / O Sun, to tell thee how I hate thy beams" (IV. 35–37). This call receives no answer. Soon the "prayer" ostensibly addressed to another turns into a solipsistic address, a soliloquy; and when Satan addresses himself rather than his Maker, he curses instead of praises: "Nay curs'd be thou; since against his thy will / Chose freely what it now so justly rues" (IV. 71–72). Praise is not so easy: "What could be less than to afford him praise" (IV. 46) whines Satan in frustration. Satan cannot envision a circumstance in which his saying would successfully issue in doing: false intentions intervene.

> But say I could repent and could obtain
> By Act of Grace my former state; how soon
> Would highth recall high thoughts, how soon unsay
> What feign'd submission swore: ease would recant
> Vows made in pain, as violent and void.
>
> (IV. 93–97)

In another violation of felicitous conditions, Satan only imagines repenting his repentence. Even the divine promise is mired in the difficulties of understanding. Just what does it mean for the heel of the woman's Seed to bruise the head of the serpent? In the final books of *Paradise Lost*, Adam has trouble getting it right. Ultimately, getting that right, understanding the meaning of the command of obedience and the meaning of the promise of salvation, is precisely the challenge Adam faces, with the world of interpretation all before him.

RITUAL RECOMPENSE

The impulse to sing in praise is expressed early in Milton's Latin poem to his father, *Ad Patrem*. He speaks of his own createdness as a gift that needs recompensing, but objects that he is inadequate to the task. He opens,

> Hoc utcunque tibi gratum, pater optime, carmen
> Exiguum meditatur opus, nec novimus ipsi
> Aptius a nobis quae possint munera donis
> Respondere tuis, quamvis nes maxima possint
> Respondere tuis, nedum ut par gratia donis
> Esse queat, vacuis quae redditur arida verbis.   (6–11)

"Yet I do not know what gifts of mine could more aptly repay yours – though my greatest gifts could never repay yours, for they cannot be equalled by any barren gratitude of futile words." Silence – failure to even begin the poetic enterprise – should logically follow such a disclaimer, but Milton brackets this sense of futility and proceeds to justify poetry. He then concludes his poem on a different note:

> At tibi, care pater, postquam non aequa merenti
> Posse referre datur, nec dona rependere factis,
> Sit memorasse satis, repetitaque munera grato
> Percensere animo, fidaeque reponere menti.   (111–14)

"But to you, dear father, since no requital equal to your desert and no deeds equal to your gifts are within my power, let it suffice that with a grateful mind I remember and tell over your constant kindnesses, and lay them up in a loyal heart." A grateful mind, *gratus animus*, discharges a debt that had seemed onerous. He ends with the hope that the song which honors his father will be an example to remote ages. While Milton may be simply opening and closing this juvenile verse with conventional shows of humility and ambition, this marked shift in tone merits attention, even at the risk of exaggerating its significance, for it is precisely this movement – from despair to confidence, from futility to gratitude, from barrenness to loyalty – that Satan considers but is unable to make.

As Satan struggles with the idea of repentence in his soliloquy, his admission that he was created instinctively prompts him to consider offering praise.

> he deserv'd no such return
> From me, whom he created what I was
> In that bright eminence, nor with his good
> Upbraided none, ...
> What could be less than to afford him praise,
> The easiest recompense, and pay him thanks,
> How due! (IV. 42–48)

But he veers away from the gesture of heavenward gratitude Adam displays at his birth. Instead, Satan's conception of gratitude becomes the subject of his discourse. Satan begins to interpret gratitude rather than to express it, activities that are antithetical. Michel de Certeau's remarks about belief also apply to praise: it

presumes and intends a doing ... you believe it if you do it, and if you do not do it you do not believe in it.... To posit the question: "Do I believe it?" is already to leave the field of belief and take it as an intellectual object independent of the act that affirms it as a relationship. Belief is no longer anything but a stating when it ceases to be a relational engaging, in other words when it ceases to be a belief.[15]

According to Satan's theory, gratitude vacillates from being an "easy recompense" to an endless burden he could never repay.

> lifted up so high
> I sdein'd subjection, and thought one step higher
> Would set me highest, and in a moment quit
> The debt immense of endless gratitude,
> So burdensome, still paying, still to owe;

Forgetful what from him I still receiv'd,
And understood not that a grateful mind
By owing owes not, but still pays, at once
Indebted and discharg'd; what burden then?   (IV. 49–57)

He depicts an awesome obligation so impossible to fulfill that failure is inevitable: he can only flee such an exacting creditor, declaring moral bankruptcy, as it were. But he concedes that this construction is a fabrication designed to justify himself when he admits to a wholly different understanding of indebtedness, "And understood not that a grateful mind / By owing owes not." Again, a grateful mind, *gratus animus*, discharges the debt, instantly and completely.

Milton's discussions of praise are dominated by the familiar language of finance, of owing, paying, and reckoning. Emile Benveniste ranks the function of the word belief (kred, credo, credit) in the category of "economic obligations," describing a sequential link from donation to remuneration. According to him, to believe is to "give away something with the certainty of getting it back."[16] Still, the "thing" exchanged is altered, if only by time, so that what is paid back is only an equivalent to what was given. His discussion of this economic exchange, this "system" of belief, centers on the role of temporality: gift and restitution must be in a sequence, must be temporally articulated for the "coming and going of the 'thing' marks, through a separation among moments, that which distinguishes its successive owners."

The "believer" abandons a present advantage, or some of its claims, to give credit to a receiver. He hollows out a void in himself relative to the time of the other, and, in the interests he calculates, he creates a deficit whereby a future is introduced into the present.[17]

And so, embedded in this most economic discourse by Satan is another preoccupation, with time. "Still" is repeated four times in this brief speech, its sense alternating between "forever," "continually," and "instantly." But with this "stillness," Satan denies the temporal relation that Benveniste describes as the character of belief. On one level, Satan is not willing to give anything up with the expectation of a return, and, unwilling to invest in his future, he denies himself one. On the other, he admits that if he were to believe, his own debt would be simultaneously incurred and discharged, that is, there would be no debt. While Benveniste begins by suggesting that belief requires a lapse of time over which credit is extended, he finally arrives at the same understanding that Satan does: for the believer, when the "future is introduced into the present," the payment has essentially been made.

Creation in sacred song

Man's greatest debt is for his greatest gift: the creation. To praise it is to discharge that debt. "A grateful recollection of the divine goodness is the first of human obligations," opens the *Second Defense of the People of England*, "and extraordinary favors demand more solemn and devout acknowledgments."[18] In *Paradise Regained*, a more trustworthy speaker echoes Satan's "easy recompense," but Christ also foresees the unhappy alternative to repaying that debt in praise.

> what could he less expect
> Than glory and benediction, that is thanks,
> The slightest, easiest, readiest recompense
> From them who could return him nothing else,
> And not returning that would likeliest render
> Contempt instead, dishonor, obloquy?
> Hard recompense, unsuitable return
> For so much good, so much beneficence.
>
> (*PR*, III. 126–33)

Christ offers no middle ground: one can either offer praise or contempt, the "easy" or the "hard recompense." Given this polarization of the options, the path Milton travels in *Ad Patrem*, from despair of adequate repayment to confidence in a just recompense, is redemptive. Praise not only discharges the debt, it benefits the giver. Herbert makes just that point in "Providence," where he casts praise in the same economic parlance.

> Wherefore, most sacred Spirit, I here present
> For me and all my fellows praise to thee:
> And just it is that I should pay the rent,
> Because the benefit accrues to me.[19]

That redemptive path – the center of *Ad Patrem* – is not devoted to confession, contrition, and repentance, but to an enumeration of the powers of poetry, "divine song." Briefly, song preserves a trace of the Promethean fire, it has the power to stir the depths of Tartarus and to bind the gods below in triple adamant; it is Priestly, for it has a ritual function in sacrifice, and it is Prophetic – the oracles of Apollo reveal the future in song. Song is our occupation in the everlasting Kingdom:

> Nos etiam, patrium tunc cum repetemus Olympum,
> Aeternaeque morae stabunt immobilis aevi,
> Ibimus auratis per caeli templa coronis,
> Dulcia suaviloquo sociantes carmina plectro,
> Astra quibus geminique poli convexa sonabunt.   (30–34)

"When we return to our native Olympus and the everlasting ages of immutable eternity are established, we shall walk, crowned with gold, through the temples of the skies and with the harp's soft accompaniment we shall sing sweet songs to which the stars shall echo and the vault of heaven from pole to pole." The list continues to include songs of heroic deeds and "of chaos and the broad foundation on which the earth rests."[20] While all of this may seem little more than a selection of conventional classical allusions to poetry, these are the very powers of song that will be elaborated and enriched to form the heart of Milton's poetic enterprise. It is all here. The vatic role of the poet;[21] the prophetic function;[22] and the Promethean spark that suggests the problem of stolen knowledge, forbidden and deserving punishment, and yet divinely inspired. The notion of song binding the gods below will also become familiar: song will silence the oracles in the Nativity Ode, and in *Paradise Lost*, that classical motif attains the dignity of a theological conviction. While the devils break loose from the triple-adamantine gates of hell (II. 646), in the end, songs of praise will seal the mouth of hell forever. Whatever the specific power of each kind of song in Milton's list, all are subsumed to that overarching purpose of praise: whatever Milton sings, he sings praise of his father in *Ad Patrem*. It is, then, the song of praise which leads Milton from despair to gratitude.

Because Satan considers praise he cannot praise, for he is already "outside" that gesture, but in *Ad Patrem*, Milton would will his song to *be* that gesture, to be "a doing". He imagines his praise joining a cosmic song, and together they will defeat the temptor.

> Spiritus et rapidos qui circinat igneus orbes
> Nunc quoque sidereis intercinit ipse choreis
> Immortale melos et inenarrabile carmen;
> Torrida dum rutilus compescit sibila serpens,
> Demissoque ferox gladio mansuescit Orion,
> Stellarum nec sentit onus Maurusius Atlas.   (35–40)

"Even now the fiery spirit who flies through the swift spheres is singing his immortal melody and unutterable song in harmony with the starry choruses. Meanwhile the shining Serpent restrains his burning hisses, fierce Orion grows gentle and drops his sword, and Mauretanian Atlas no longer feels the load of the stars." *Ad Patrem* sings of a myth of presumption: Phaethon riding the sun's chariot is threatened by the Serpent, causing him to lose control (*Metamorphoses*, II, 173–75), but song restrains the Serpent. Orion's sword, which "frightened the stars" in Statius (Silv. I:44–45), is laid down

here, gently, again by song. By its very content, the song of
gratitude foils the temptation to offer dishonor, obloquy. Simply
put, remembering and telling over defeats the temptation to forget.

Such song echoes throughout *Paradise Lost*. Not only do "millions
of spiritual Creatures walk the Earth / Unseen," continually praising
the creation, so do Adam and Eve. Their aubade, based on Psalm
148 and Psalm 19, offers the vision of every created thing joining
in a great hymn of praise to creation. A natural congregation
performs a spontaneous worship service.

> Speak yee who best can tell, ye Sons of Light,
> Angels, for yee behold him, and with songs
> And choral symphonies, Day without Night,
> Circle his Throne rejoicing, yee in Heav'n;
> On Earth join all ye Creatures to extol
> Him first, him last, him midst, and without end.
>
> (V. 160–65)

The hymn continues with the sun, the fixt stars, the air, the elements
that "mix / And nourish all things, let your ceaseless change / Vary
to our great Maker still new praise" and mists, plants, fountains,
birds. Finally, it includes an allusion to the serpent.

> Yee that in Waters glide, and yee that walk
> The Earth, and stately tread, or lowly creep;
>
> (V. 200–01)

While all the creatures are included here, specified, as in Genesis,
by their mode of locomotion, Milton highlights the serpent "that
lowly creeps" with the emphatic end-stop position. There are other
not-so-veiled allusions to the Tempter in the aubade. The morning
star is asked to praise.

> Fairest of Stars, last in the train of Night,
> If better thou belong not to the dawn,
> Sure pledge of day, that crown'st the smiling Morn
> With thy bright Circlet, praise him in thy Sphere
> While day arises, that sweet hour of Prime.
>
> (V. 166–70)

Lucifer is no longer the last star of night; he is the "sure pledge of
day." The effect is to dispel the very possibility of a Tempter through
hymn – to co-opt the tempting voice and turn it to praise – for
the song imaginatively supplies the gratitude which the morning star
refuses to offer. The aubade describes the course of the sun with
equally allusive language: its journey reads like a moral allegory.

Thou Sun, of this great World both Eye and Soul,
Acknowledge him thy Greater, sound his praise
In thy eternal course, both when thou climb'st,
And when high Noon hast gain'd, and when thou fall'st.

(V. 171–74, my emphasis)

The temporal danger-zones, the hour of temptation and fall, are
"neutralized," for any threat is dispelled with ceaseless praise.
Finally, the hymn concludes with a command in imitation of that
first one, "Let there be light":

... and if the night
Have gather'd aught of evil or conceal'd,
Disperse it, as now light dispels the dark.

(V. 206–08)

The aubade is the most explicit expression of praise in the epic
and Milton presents it at a critical dramatic moment: the morning
after Eve's temptation dream. With their celebration of creation
following close upon Eve's tears of repentance and Adam's gesture
of forgiveness – wiping those tears from her eyes – the song of
praise serves, symbolically, as a final cleansing of the poisoned
atmosphere. That narrative context recapitulates the hymn's internal
drama: the aubade dispels the demon of the night. The scene recalls
the wiping of tears in *Lycidas*, a consolation by the shepherd which
also issues in song, the "unexpressive nuptual song" of the creation
in Revelation.

Worthy art thou, our Lord and God,
to receive glory and honor and power,
for thou didst create all things,
and by thy will they existed and were created.

(Rev. 4:11)

In *Lycidas*, praise of creation would dispel a similar temptation: to
despair.

As Adam and Eve join their voices to a hymn of praise sung by
all of the created works, so the act of creation itself is virtually sung,
rather than spoken, into existence. The injunction concluding *Ad
Patrem* to "remember and tell over" his earthly father's kindnesses
also prescribes Milton's response to the "kindness" of his heavenly
Father, not just for his birth, but for the birth of the universe. Each
act of creation is rehearsed and remembered upon its completion,
its celebration following so close upon the event that the first "birthday party" takes place at the birth itself.

Creation in sacred song

> Thus was the first Day Ev'n and Morn:
> Nor pass'd uncelebrated, nor unsung
> By the Celestial Choirs, when Orient Light
> Exhaling first from Darkness they beheld;
> Birth-day of Heav'n and Earth; with joy and shout
> The hollow Universal Orb they fill'd,
> And touch'd thir Golden Harps, and hymning prais'd
> God and his works, Creator him they sung,
> Both when first Ev'ning was, and when first Morn.
>
> (VII. 252–60)

With harps and hymns, the very act of creation becomes a worship service.

This impulse to commemorate the event ritually even as it occurs has Biblical precedent. In Genesis, the creation narrative includes the provision for its own commemoration: the sabbath. "So God blessed the seventh day and hallowed it, because on it God rested from all his work which he had done in creation" (Gen. 2:3). And so it is prescribed, "Remember the sabbath day, to keep it holy. Six days you shall labor, and do all your work; but the seventh day is a sabbath to the Lord our God; ... for in six days the Lord made heaven and earth, the sea, and all that is in them, and rested the seventh day; therefore the Lord blessed the sabbath day and hallowed it" (Ex. 20:8–11). Furthermore, the form of the Priestly creation narrative itself is liturgical. The periodization of time marking Genesis 1 has likened it to a festal week and its repetitive *qui tov* ("it was good") rings like the refrain of a hymn. The periodic repetitions – "and it was evening, and it was morning" – have even invited Biblical scholars to speculate that the present form of the narrative reflects many generations of liturgical use; one scholar believes that the Priestly story was rehearsed confessionally to glorify the God of Israel.[23] Milton need not have access to such cultic history in order to be sensitive to the liturgical character of this creation account. Creation and liturgy are deeply linked; Ricoeur understands them as inseparable.

The first entrance of the drama of creation into the History of men is the cult and the ensemble of ritual practices that surround all human activities. Now the cult is already a kind of action – not only a fictive re-enactment, but a renewal of the drama by active participation. Mankind, says the creation-myth, was created for the service of the gods, ... and this service ... calls for the real re-enactment of the drama of creation.[24]

Ricoeur's remarks about the magnitude of the Babylonian New Year's festival shed light on Milton's creation festival, the sabbath.

With harps and hymns, Milton's rest is not silent; rather, it reenacts
the first celebration of the creation.

> the Harp
> Had work and rested not, the solemn Pipe,
> And Dulcimer, all Organs of sweet stop,
> All sounds on Fret by String or Golden Wire
> Temper'd soft Tunings, intermixt with Voice
> Choral or Unison; of incense Clouds
> Fuming from Golden Censers hid the Mount.
> Creation and the Six days' acts they sung: (VII. 594–601)

All creatures join Adam and Eve in a daily hymn of praise,
millions of unseen spirits continually sing praises antiphonally; the
creation is depicted and continually celebrated with the richest
possible liturgy. Milton has clearly devised an extensive liturgy of
praise to form the backdrop to the action of *Paradise Lost*, one designed
to make his praise a ritual "doing" rather than a "stating."[25] Set
over against the events of temptation and fall, this hymn of praise
functions in the same way that praise functions in the aubade – as
an antidote to temptation. Praise is sung in the poem whether Adam
and Eve, like the sun, "climbst" or when "high Noon hast gain'd,
and when [they] fall" (V. 173, 74). Heedless of passing events subject
to the exigencies of time, this incessant ritual has the effect of
transcending time, for all time is made present in ritual. A ritually
celebrated creation did not occur once-upon-a-time, in a moment
in history, but in mythical time, "in illo tempore." In his exploration
of rituals concerning creation, Eliade also discusses the Babylonian
Akitu festival, concluding that

all rituals imitate a divine archetype and that their continual reactualization
takes place in one and the same atemporal mythical instant ... [Such
ceremonies] suspend the flow of profane time, of duration, and project the
celebrant into a mythical time, *in illo tempore*.[26]

Creation is continual, not an original event that is opposed to
repetition, but a constant reaffirmation of divine initiative, one
"answered" by the human song. To rehearse the creation is to reenact it.[27] As celebrant, Milton does not discover a privileged
beginning; he re-creates beginnings.[28]

The opulence of Milton's liturgy is striking. This is no spare
Puritan metrical psalm. Rather, Milton indulges his obvious delight
in the elaborateness of church ornament to the fullest. Measured
against Puritan principles of austerity in worship, Milton commits
an appalling display of excess. Harp, pipe, organs, voices in chorus

and unison, and even incense comprise Milton's creation liturgy, in contrast to the somber sabbath Du Bartas depicts.

> For, by th'Almightie this great Holy-day
> Was not ordain'd to daunce, and maske, and play ...
> God would, that men should in a certaine place
> This Day assemble as before his face,
> Lending an humble and attentive eare
> To learne his great Names deere-dread loving-feare.[29]

William Prynne would eliminate all church music, for it only distracts from the matter at hand: instruction.[30] John Vicars was delighted when the organ music and antiphonal singing were silenced in Westminster Abbey in 1649, both to be replaced by a daily sermon. "The *bellowing* Organs are demolisht and pull'd down, the *treble* or rather *trouble* and base singers, Chanters or Inchanters driven out; and instead thereof, there is now a most blessed Orthodox Preaching Ministry."[31] Milton's own anti-liturgical remarks, if less vituperative, are no less emphatic. In the *Apology*, he challenges liturgy in the name of scripture.

Like therefore as the retaining of this Romish Liturgy is a provocation to God, and a dishonour to our Church, so is it by those ceremonies, those purifyings and offrings at the Altar, a pollution and disturbance to the Gospell itselfe; and a kind of driving us with the foolish *Galatians* to another gospell. (*CP*, 1, 941)

In *Eikonoclastes*, he defends an ordinance which substitutes the simplified *Directory* for the Book of Common Prayer and forbids the use of any other form of worship on penalty of a year's imprisonment for a third offense (*CP*, 3, 508). He depicts liturgy as a servile yoke, oppressing the freedom of heartfelt piety.

For the manner of using sett formes, there is no doubt but that, wholesom matter, and good desires rightly conceav'd in the heart, wholesom words will follow of themselves. Neither can any true Christian find a reason why Liturgie should be at all admitted, a prescription not impos'd or practis'd by those first Founders of the Church, who alone had that autority: Without whose precept or example, how constantly the Priest puts on his Gown and Surplice, so constantly doth his praier put on a servile yoak of Liturgie.
(*CP*, 3, 504–05)

What are we to make of the discrepancy between the architectonic, almost Catholic, liturgy forming the substructure of the epic and Milton the Puritan's opposition to it in prose? The conflict is a specious one. When Milton celebrates the creation with choirs and harps and incense, he is neither forgetting nor bracketing a sentiment he holds elsewhere. The creation is too important. The liturgy is too insistent. In *De Doctrina*, the issue devolves to the distinction between external and internal worship. "External worship, moreover, though it may be distinguished from internal for sake of argument, should in practice go hand in hand with it, and the two are never separated except by the viciousness of sinners" (*CP*, 6, 666). Milton objects to a *separated* worship; no external form can suffice as substitute for "internal or spiritual involvement." The separation between external and internal worship only occurs after the fall; it is, in fact, one of the tragic signs of moral degeneration.

> the rest, far greater part,
> Will deem in outward Rites and specious forms
> Religion satisfi'd; Truth shall retire
> Bestuck with sland'rous darts, and works of Faith
> Rarely be found: so shall the World go on,
> To good malignant, to bad men benign,
> Under her own weight groaning, ... (XII. 533 – 39)

Milton collects the Biblical injunctions against the sanctuary and false sacrifice, prominent among them: "The sacrifice of the wicked is an abomination to the Lord" (Prov. 15:8), and "Do not trust in these deceptive words: 'This is the temple of the Lord, the temple of the Lord, the temple of the Lord' " (Jer. 7:4), but then he asserts the corollary conviction that true worship is acceptable to God, whatever form it assumes. With his Deity, Milton prefers "Before all Temples th' upright heart and pure" (*CP*, 1, 18). But before the fall – at the creation – he need not make a choice. It *is* the upright heart that sings antiphonally, that plays the organ, that carries incense – as the obedient angels testify. Milton takes the trappings of liturgy and lifts them out of the institution. Tearing down the wall of the temple, he re-erects the Temple in the cosmos instead.

The mythology is already in place, Milton need only turn it, as ever, to his purpose. He understands the "whorish harmony" of the church, as Prynne so delicately phrases it, as becoming cosmic harmony – the music of the spheres. The association seems inevitable. Milton's interest in *harmonia mundi* is attested as early as his academic exercise, the *Second Prolusion*. There he speaks with irony of taking up a new, rather than a commonplace subject, traces the sources of the tradition to Pythagoras and Plato, and concludes with the conviction that our own inability to hear the music of the spheres is the fault of Prometheus' theft of fire (*CP*, 1, 234 – 39). In *At a Solemn Music*, he makes the Christian analogue explicit. With the fall, the universal harmony is broken, the cosmic liturgy silenced, and it will only be restored with our redemption.

> disproportion'd sin
> Jarr'd against nature's chime, and with harsh din
> Broke the fair music that all creatures made
> To their great Lord, whose love their motion sway'd
> In perfect Diapason, whilst they stood
> In first obedience and their state of good.
> O may we soon again renew that Song,
> And keep in tune with Heav'n, till God ere long
> To his celestial consort us unite,
> To live with him, and sing in endless morn of light.
>
> (At a Solemn Music, 19 – 28)

If the theft of Prometheus and Adam breaks the music, Pythagoras, who was sent "to instruct mankind in holiness and lead them back to righteousness" can hear the music of the spheres (in the Second Prolusion CP, 1, 238).[32] The distinction between forbidden and divine knowledge surfaces again: Milton would join Pythagoras in his hope to confer divine knowledge, not the forbidden, stolen knowledge of Prometheus. As he would see and tell, so would he hear that music and empower us to hear it.

COSMIC LITURGY

John Hollander and Leo Spitzer have both traced the harmonia mundi tradition and while their approaches are different – Hollander unpacks the poetry of two centuries while Spitzer's primary tool is philological – both conclude that as governing metaphor, cosmic music fuses the theological, epistemological, and scientific assumptions of an age, that the unravelling of that metaphor represents no less than the disintegration of a world view.[33] The spirit of "medieval godliness" is deadened with the destruction of musica mundana. It is in the seventeenth century, according to Hollander, that the sky is untuned, and Spitzer writes,

The history of the disappearance of the one field (world harmony – well temperedness) is simply the history of modern civilization, of the Weberian "Entzauberung der Welt" or dechristianization [a process that] ... began in the seventeenth century and was completed in the eighteenth.[34]

Milton represents not so much the last gasp as the majestic culmination of the tradition. It is still unbroken in this militant Protestant: in *On the Morning of Christ's Nativity* (IX – XIV), the ancient idea of World Harmony is "harmonized" with Christ's birth, and in a manner not essentially different from that characteristic of the Middle Ages – except, perhaps, acoustically, the colossal world-organ voice of Milton resounds in nine-fold harmony.[35]

There *is* something essentially different about Milton's use of the tradition – but not his flaunting of the Puritan bias against music – commentators on the psalms found ample occasion to pull out the organ stops. Wither prefaces his *Preparation to the Psalter* with a lyric that imagines a universal hymn, joined by the spheres, answered by a divine blessing that issues in a full-voiced quire that will drive the fiends to hell. Apparently, the association of cosmic harmony with the hymn of praise is not original either.[36]

> From the *Earth's* vast hollow woombe
> *Musick's* deepest Base shall come,
> Seas, and Flouds, from Shore to Shore,
> Shall the Counter-Tenour roare.
> To this Consort (when we sing)
> Whistling winds, your Descant bring:
> Which may beare the sound above,
> Where the Orbe of Fire doth move;
> And so climbe, from Spheare to Spheare,
> Till our Song Th'Almightie heare.
>
> So shall *He*, from Heaven's high Towre,
> On the Earth his Blessing showre:
> All this huge wide Orbe we see,
> Shall one *Quire*, one *Temple* be.
> There our voices we will reare,
> Till we fill it every where;
> And enforce the *Fiends*, that dwell
> In the Aire, to sink in Hell.
> Then, O Come; With sacred Laies,
> Let us sound Th'Almightie's Praise.[37]

What *is* distinctive is the place accorded the world harmony tradition in those Miltonic themes of trial and temptation, indebtedness and gratitude, memory and liturgy, and the distinctly Miltonic myth that unites them. That heavenly music, denied to us in our disobedience, was once audible to the unfallen Adam, as Raphael pointedly reminds him in the midst of his creation account.

>   Up he rode
> Follow'd with acclamation and the sound
> Symphonious of ten thousand Harps that tun'd
> Angelic harmonies: the Earth, the Air
> Resounded, (thou remember'st, for thou heard'st)
> The Heav'ns and all the Constellations rung,
>
>   (VII. 557–62)

Ritual remembering and reenactment multiply: we have seen that the creation is commemorated even as it comes into being; now Adam is reminded of its commemorative song – even as the creation is recounted to him. Creation is reenacted for Adam in three senses: by the music he once heard, by the present narration of Raphael, and by the *memory* of the song, a perpetual memory that makes him, like Urania and Wisdom, a continual witness to the creation. To hear the music of the spheres is to remember the creation, to recall contingency, to pay back in gratitude, and to recreate. For Milton, a universe conceived in song is one which repays its own debt, binds up any discordant threat to its destruction, restrains the hisses of the serpent and lays down the sword of Orion – gently – in sweet harmony. It is a universe that justifies itself.

This logic is brilliantly, if breathlessly, condensed in *On the Morning of Christ's Nativity*. As Milton explains in both the "Sixth Elegy" and the preludium to the Ode, he offers a hymn of praise as his gift.

> Dona quidem dedimus Christi natalibus illa;
> Illa sub auroram lux mihi prima tulit.
> ("Sixth Elegy," 87–88)

"These are my gifts for the birthday of Christ – gifts which the first light of its dawn brought to me." The humble song of praise soon swells into an elaborate liturgy, on the order of the service accompanying the creation in *Paradise Lost*.

> Ring out ye Crystal spheres,
> Once bless our human ears,
>   (If ye have power to touch our senses so)
> And let your silver chime
> Move in melodious time;
>   And let the Bass of Heav'n's deep Organ blow,
> And with your ninefold harmony
> Make up full consort to th'Angelic symphony.
> (*On the Morning of Christ's Nativity*, stanza XIII)

Much is contained in that parenthetical question. In *At a Solemn Music* and *Arcades*, Milton tells us that *if* we could hear that music, as Adam once did, we would be redeemed. Here he asks if the universal liturgy itself somehow can empower us to be auditors, if the cosmic song itself can enact rather than describe, redeeming us in what is essentially an act of grace. Early in his career, then, Milton made redemption depend upon song's power to perform: "if ye have power to touch our senses so." His answer was not a resounding yes; rather, he maintained the conditional. Like the aubade of Adam and Eve, the holy song in the Nativity Ode can defeat demons, "*if* such holy song / Enwrap our fancy long." Language could have no greater power, and, as a result, the difficulties which attend it could have no more dire consequences.

> For if such holy Song
> Enwrap our fancy long,
>   Time will run back, and fetch the age of gold,
> And speckl'd vanity
> Will sicken soon and die,
>   And leprous sin will melt from earthly mold,
> And Hell itself will pass away,
> And leave her dolorous mansions to the peering day.
>
>   (stanza XIV)

This hymn – that could dissolve hell, make us present at the birth of Christ, and enable us to be redeemed at the end of time (if we could hear it) – was heard once before, at the Beginning (as 'tis said). The status of that original song is also problematic, for knowledge of it must be mediated.

> Such Music (as 'tis said)
> Before was never made,
>   But when of old the sons of morning sung,
> While the Creator Great
> His constellations set,
>   And the well-balanc't world on hinges hung,
> And cast the dark foundations deep,
> And bid the welt'ring waves their oozy channel keep.
>
>   (stanza XII)

The "sons of morning" is an allusion to Job 38. With that key reference, Milton joins the *locus classicus* for Biblical song to the classical *harmonia mundi*:

> Where were you when I laid the foundation of the earth?
> Tell me, if you have understanding.
> Who determined its measurements – surely you know!
> Or who stretched the line upon it?
> On what were its bases sunk, or who laid its cornerstone,
> When the morning stars sang together,
> And all the sons of God shouted for joy?   (Job 38:4–7)

Milton's myth of divine song crystallizes around this reference to Job's theodicy. Of all his Biblical models, Job is the one in which the theodical issue is most pressing, the one that could offer itself, not only as a generic model for the "brief epic," *Paradise Regained*,[38] but as a thematic example for "the little Bible," *Paradise Lost*.

God entered a wager that allowed "the Adversary" to tempt Job;
Milton's Satan could not rear his head from the fiery flood without
the "will / And high permission of all-ruling Heaven" (I. 212). And
when Job asks why – as Milton simply puts it, "what cause?" –
the voice from the whirlwind gives the answer: "I am the Creator."

In Job, and wherever the creation is invoked in the Bible, the twin
impulses of human contingency and divine majesty find expression.
The sequence in Genesis 1 suggests that man is both the last of
creatures and the crown of creation; however diminished in the context of the vast cosmos, he is, nonetheless, the only creature made in
the image of God. The paradox is summarized in Psalm 8:

> When I look at thy heavens, the work of thy fingers,
> the moon and the stars which thou hast established;
> what is man that thou art mindful of him,
> and the son of man that thou dost care for him?
> Yet thou hast made him little less than God,
> and dost crown him with glory and honor.
> Thou hast given him dominion over the works of thy hands;
> thou hast put all things under his feet,   (Ps. 8:3–6)

Augustine invokes these twin impulses at the opening of his
Confessions.

*Can any praise be worthy of the Lord's majesty? How magnificent his strength! How
inscrutable his wisdom!* Man is one of your creatures, Lord, and his instinct
is to praise you. He bears about him the mark of death, the sign of his own
sin, to remind him that you *thwart the proud*. But still, since he is a part of
your creation, he wishes to praise you.[39]

There could be no clearer statement of the answer to Job, no more
eloquent expression of the logic informing Milton's theodicy.
Creation inspires praise, man's "instinct" and his "wish," and
praise – when it works – redeems "the mark of death."[40]

Two classic studies of the Nativity Ode fragment this logic. Arthur
Barker divides the poem into thirds: "The first eight stanzas ...
describe the setting of the Nativity, the next nine the angelic choir,
the next nine the flight of the heathen gods."[41] A. S. P. Woodhouse
distinguishes the "aesthetic center" (the music of the spheres) from
the "intellectual core" (the routing of the heathen gods by Christ),
only hinting at their relation.[42] Without needing to reunify a work
he has not fragmented, Edward W. Tayler reads the poem as
organized around a single controlling idea.[43] Referring to Barker's
emphasis on image patterns and Woodhouse's isolation of an
"intellectual core," Tayler subordinates both to what he believes

is the main theme of the Nativity Ode: time. He demonstrates how the tenses in the poem, the use of "now" and Biblical typology (Milton abruptly reverts to the past, to Sinai, to refer to the future, the Last Judgment) all contribute to transcending linear time in order to make the past present. Milton "organizes the poem on the basis of principles of scriptural exegesis rather than on congeries, associationist or other, of images." The introductory stanzas portray Milton on Christmas morn of 1629 looking back to the first Christmas, but by the fourth stanza, those times are conflated: Milton will present his ode to the Infant before the Wiseman.

> The "Now" of the Nativity Ode may therefore also be considered a poetic *nunc stans*, glancing simultaneously toward present and past and conflating the two events separated in Time as though viewed from the vantage of Eternity.... This meaningful "confusion," familiar to readers of the Christian poetry of the Middle Ages and Renaissance, stems from an awareness that the principal events of history occur but once and yet are "repeated" – in the life of each Christian and throughout the holy days of the church calendar.[44]

In the Nativity Ode, Tayler discovers an understanding of ritual time and repetition that also characterizes Milton's approach to creation in *Paradise Lost*. I would only add that we heed the ritual *form* Milton chose to represent his typology. Milton's choice of the hymn is crucial, for it is the hymn which may be empowered to make "time run back and fetch the age of gold," the hymn that might ultimately unite us to God's "celestial consort," "To live with him, and sing [a hymn] in endless morn of light." Milton would grant the hymn a status not accorded to other discourse; he would have it not simply *interpret* time typologically, but *enact* typology, drawing singer and auditor into those events as participants. It is no wonder, then, that Milton would join his voice "unto the Angel Choir" not only in the Nativity Ode, but also in his other early lyrics which share the fiction of mortals on earth singing a hymn together with the angels.[45] Nervousness about the efficacy of hymn surfaces throughout: in "Upon the Circumcision" the hymn "erst" was sung; "At a Solemn Music" expresses the wish to renew the broken song; and in "The Passion," the hymn fails utterly.

In *Paradise Lost*, that fiction of the poet's song joining the angel choir is elaborated in Book III. The proclamation of the providential plan to elevate the Son is celebrated in sacred song.

> with Preamble sweet
> Of charming symphony they introduce
> Thir sacred Song, and waken raptures high;
> No voice exempt, no voice but well could join
> Melodious part, such concord is in Heav'n.   (III. 367–71)

The hymn concludes with the subtle shift from "their" song to the personal pronoun.

> Hail Son of God, Savior of Men, thy Name
> Shall be the copious matter of *my* Song
> Henceforth, and never shall my Harp thy praise
> Forget, nor from thy Father's praise disjoin.
> (III. 412–15, my emphasis)

That shift has two opposite implications, ones that never resolve. Perhaps Milton's imaginative power to hear the angelic choir has collapsed and he can only offer his own voice instead. On the other hand, the subtle insertion of his voice could signal that Milton's song has merged with the angelic choir rather than replaced it. Editors have noted that the second half of Book III itself begins with the angelic hymn just as the first half began with the poet's own hymn, the invocation to light.[46] In Book III, then, Milton has composed an antiphonal hymn to convey sacred history. The method is applicable to the poem at large. *Paradise Lost* would not only include hymns; it would constitute one.

PARADISE LOST AS HYMN

Milton stretches every genre to its utmost limit. *Lycidas* may begin as pastoral elegy, but the impulse to break out of the strictures of its convention continually surfaces: "That strain I heard was of a higher mood" (l. 87), "Return Alpheus, the dread voice is past" (l. 131). The humble pastoral oaten flute is called upon to accommodate such unpastoral images as the two-handed engine of the Last Judgment. As pastoral aspires to prophecy in *Lycidas*, so in *Paradise Lost*, the epic would swell into a hymn. If *Paradise Lost* discharges Milton's debt, it is as hymn; if the temptation to forget is defeated, it is by hymn; and if presumption can be turned into confession, it is through hymn. When he joins Augustine in praise, "I do acknowledge you, Lord of heaven and earth, and I praise you for my first beginnings, although I can not remember them,"[47] Milton would distinguish himself from the Satan who refuses to praise and who "remember'st not" his making. The liturgical backdrop to *Paradise Lost* is, then, no mere background, and the epic is not adequately depicted as

"Law and Story strew'd with hymn." Rather, set over and against the linear action which, however displaced, still unravels into an ascertainable sequence of events, the hymn offers another sense of time, ritual time. The hymn that is *Paradise Lost* makes time run backward to creation and forward to redemption, as it does in the Nativity Ode, holding forth redemption even at the moment of the fall – as in the aubade. The hymn of Adam and Eve is explicitly made the exemplum for the epic itself. The preface to their prayer is our best evidence that *Paradise Lost* was conceived as a kind of prayer.[48]

> Lowly they bow'd adoring, and began
> Thir Orisons, each Morning duly paid
> In various style, for neither various style
> Nor holy rapture wanted they to praise
> Thir Maker, in fit strains pronounct or sung
> Unmeditated, such prompt eloquence
> Flow'd from thir lips, in Prose or numerous Verse,
> More tuneable than needed Lute or Harp
> To add more sweetness, and thus they began.
>
> (V. 144–52)

A simplified liturgy, with no need for orchestration, but a liturgy nonetheless. Milton's longer hymn, *Paradise Lost*, sung "in various style," in "unpremeditated verse," in "fit strains" for a fit audience, is no less liturgical.[49] The first parents conclude with the prayer that

>   if the night
> Have gather'd aught of evil or conceal'd,
> Disperse it, as now light dispels the dark.   (V. 206–8)

And Milton's own hymn opens with the prayer to disperse the evil of his night, "What in me is dark, illumine."

To speak of the hymnic character of the epic is not to mix categories carelessly. The psalm has long been seen as the model for Herbert's poetry, with Lewalski, among others, claiming that Herbert "undertakes nothing less than the task of becoming a Christian psalmist, transposing (as he indicates in 'Easter') the elements of biblical art upon a Christian lute resounding in harmony with Christ's cross."[50] Such broad analogies have not been often drawn to *Paradise Lost*.[51] Its epic, rather than lyric form is doubtless responsible for this hesitation, but that caution falls away when we focus on the function of the poem. Alongside the Renaissance preoccupation with genre theory and the immense energy devoted to categorizing Biblical literature according to classical kinds, a corollary aspect of that work took place. In addition to conferring literary distinctions upon the Bible, Milton invested his literature with a Biblical understanding of dynamic language. If Milton were to look for a precedent for his attempt to create a sacred utterance, he would look to the Bible; if he sought a model for praise, he would look to the Book of Praises, *Sepher Tehillim*, the psalms. The psalms could teach him something about epic, not only because they describe an embedded "drama of the soul," but because in another sense, they are not interested in describing a drama at all, but in enacting piety, in praising. However artful their form, the psalms were not simply a "literary" work for Milton. Conversely, *Paradise Lost* may best be understood as an "epic psalter." On the subject of genre, Raymond Waddington judiciously but safely concludes,

Milton's poetry exhibits all the late Renaissance tendencies toward generic mixture and inclusiveness; but, however much he modifies the conventional limits of a poetic kind, his works have a firm, governing generic identity. *Paradise Lost*, as a simulacrum of God's own creation, contains all things; and literary inclusiveness is a strategy of the poet's plenitude. But while we recognize the local effects of emblem and hymn, Petrarchan love lyric and Platonic dialogue, and respond to the larger modal movements of pastoral to tragedy, all this is firmly contained by the enveloping epic form.[52]

Clearly his notion of hymn, of psalm, is constricted to the narrowest possible sense. We have seen that the effects of hymn are not local.

Milton could also find in classical genre theory a closer association between epic and hymn than we might recognize. According to Aristotle's theory of the origin of poetry, epic is derived from hymn, both being forms of praise.[53] Looking back to Plato, Renaissance commentators discovered the priority he gave to hymn. While he banished poets from his Republic, condemning their fictions for leading men to vice, he exempts "Hymns to the gods and praises of famous men" (X. 607). "It will be proper to have hymns and praises of the gods intermingled with prayers, and after the gods, prayers and praises should be offered to demigods and heroes, suitable to their several characters" (Laws, 80). Similarly, to understand Milton's epic as "rising" to the strains of hymn is not to invert their hierarchy arbitrarily. The question of the relative rank of epic and hymn is not so neatly settled. O. B. Hardison argues that the commonly presumed ranking – (1) epic (2) dramatic (3) lyric – did not prevail among Renaissance theorists after all; rather, "there was a good deal of controversy over the relative merits of the three."

Critics who followed Plato and Aristotle in deriving poetry from hymns to the gods ... tended [conveniently] to ignore Aristotle's belief that evolution is a progressive movement from lower to higher forms and to rank hymn as the highest of all forms of poetry. It was generally conceded when the matter arose that the psalms are the most excellent of all poems and David the prince of poets.[54]

Puttenham is one such spokesman in *The Arte of English Poesie*.

[T]hese hymnes to the gods was the first forme of Poesie and the highest & the stateliest, & they were song by the Poets as priests, and by the people or whole congregation, as we sing in our Churches the Psalmes of *David*.[55]

Sidney praises the figurative language of the psalms.[56] George Wither said the Psalter was the "most excellent Lyricke Poesy that ever was invented."[57] The explosion of metrical versions of the psalms (there were 320 editions of metrical psalms in England alone before 1640),[58] the legion commentaries on the psalms, and the debt to the psalms in the poetry of the period[59] make their importance in the seventeenth century difficult to overdraw. As Coburn Freer describes it: "the metrical psalm was as much a movement as a genre."[60]

In the *Reason of Church Government*, Milton couples Biblical to classical precedent in his discussion of generic distinctions, and in the oft-quoted passage where he cites Job as a "brief model" for the epic, the Song of Solomon as an example of "divine pastoral Drama," and the Apocalypse of St. John as "the majestick image of a high and stately Tragedy," he concludes with the Biblical lyric.

those magnifick Odes and Hymns wherein *Pindarus* and *Callimachus* are in most things worthy, some others in their frame judicious, in their matter most an end faulty: But those frequent songs throughout the law and prophets beyond all these, not in their divine argument alone, but in the very critical art of composition may be easily made appear over all the kinds of Lyrick poesy, to be incomparable. (*CP*, 1, 815–16)

In *Paradise Regained*, Christ corrects literary history to assert the priority of the psalms over classical poetry.

> All our Law and Story strew'd
> With Hymns, our Psalms with artful terms inscrib'd
> Our Hebrew Songs and Harps in *Babylon*,
> That pleas'd so well our Victors' ear, declare
> That rather *Greece* from us these Arts deriv'd; (IV. 334–38)

Even where Milton inveighs against external worship, he exempts the psalms, for psalms are not only found in scripture, the singing of psalms is prescribed there.

Invocation, and particularly thanksgiving, is some times accompanied by singing and by hymns in honor of the divine name. Mark xiv. 26: *when they had sung a hymn*; Eph v. 19–20: *speaking to one another in psalms and hymns and spiritual songs, singing and making music in your hearts, to the Lord, giving thanks ...*; Col. iii. 16: *teaching and admonishing one another in psalms and hymns ...*; James v. 13: *is anyone glad at heart? Let him sing psalms.*

(*CP*, 6, 669, Milton's ellipses)

Finally, as if to clear all doubt on the matter, the anonymous biographer has left us the last word: "David's Psalms were held in esteem with him above all poetry."[61]

Nonetheless, to separate the psalm from other forms and to elevate it instead is equally misguided in the end. In the seventeenth century, the psalm was spoken of with the same language of inclusiveness that Waddington reserves for epic. The psalm was perceived, not as one among many genres, but as a meta-genre, itself subject to a range of systems of classification. Most notably, Wither felt the need to use a variety of verse forms in his translation of the psalms, "*Because* Prayers, Praises, Lamentations, Tryumphs, *and subjects which are* Pastoral, Heroical, Elegiacall, and mixt (*all which are found in the* Psalmes) *are not properly exprest in one sort of* Measure."[62] In his sermons, Donne analyzed the types of psalms according to their titles. His major division is between psalms of prayer and of praise. But ultimately even that distinction breaks down as both are subsumed to the overriding purpose of praise.

The Book is Praise, the parts are Prayer. The name changes not the nature; Prayer and Praise is the same thing ... the duties agree in the heart and mouth of a man ... Gods house in this world is called the house of Prayer; but in heaven it is the house of Praise.[63]

According to Lewalski, the psalms were generally seen as a compendium of all the modes of divine revelation, "law, prophecy, history, proverbs; of all the emotion and passions of the human soul;" and of all genres and styles.[64] Outdoing Waddington's notion of epic inclusiveness, Luther spoke of the Book of Psalms as "a little Bible; for in it all things that are contained in the Bible are ... condensed into a most beautiful manual."[65] It is, then, in this broad sense that the "little Bible" serves as a model for Milton's own.

Radzinowicz remarks that "the Milton family combined verse and voice, and because they united them to the service of religion they were nearly indifferent to whether an extremely gifted son should be pastor or poet so long as voice and verse were biblically inspired and the life of the poet or pastor religiously directed."[66] Milton never conceived of his poetry as secular; rather, he tried to write "divine song." His liturgical vocation is not lost, it is only deflected. Milton may well have harbored the ambition to contribute to the religious life of England through a national psalter translation,[67] and perhaps that hope translated into his epic-psalter. His early commitment to "celebrate in glorious and lofty hymns the throne and equipage of God's almightiness" awaited the proper setting; Milton's Book of Praises to creation had to grow out of the context of chaos, of a curse of "death and woe." If *Paradise Lost* is a psalm, it is sung by Job.

To the Biblical forebears of Milton, the prophets and priests, the chosen "Shepherd, who first taught ... In the Beginning the Heav'ns and Earth rose out of chaos," and to Job, we must add the figure of David the psalmist. David calms the mad Saul with his lyre, as Milton eases the chaos of his world with his psalm. And yet, for all of Milton's recourse to the psalms, he makes little mention of David explicitly.[68] In a period when references to David are rife, from Marvell to Cowley, that slight is noteworthy. Milton turns far more frequently to David's classical analogue: in Miltonic typology, where pagan and Biblical traditions are continuous, Orpheus becomes a "type" of David. He too was an inspired singer, soothing the "stony and beastly people," according to Sidney.[69] The analogy between David and Orpheus was made explicit in the Renaissance, by Ficino and by Pico della Mirandola.[70] Marot dedicates his *Pseaumes*, 1541:

> N'a il souvent au doulx son de sa lyre
> Bien appaisé de Dieu courroucé l'ire?
> N'en a il pas souvent de ces bas lieux
> Les escoutans ravy jusques aux cieulx
> Et faict cesser de Saül la manie
> Pendant le temps que duroit l'armonie?
>   Si Orpheus jadis l'eust entendue,
> La sienne il eust à quelque arbre pendue;[71]

Guy Lefevre de la Boderie wrote his motto at the beginning and end of his publications: "May Holy David sprout forth as One orphically" and in a long poem he juxtaposed translations of Orphic fragments and the psalms "in order to show that the same God inspired both."[72] The appeal of Orpheus to the Renaissance is apparent: he came down from tradition as the one who civilized barbarians with culture. Milton's own attraction to the figure is equally clear, as prophet, poet, *theologis* – one who sings of the gods and the origins of the world – and sufferer. That last quality may well be the key to Milton's choice of the pagan singer over the

Hebrew one. There could be many explanations for Milton's preference of Orpheus to David; among them, that the identification of Cromwell with David the King had preempted Milton's own association with David as poet. But the selection of Orpheus carries other weight. While David suffered, he did not endure dismemberment in final defeat. His song, the psalter, was not drowned by the savage clamor.

Milton is not simply attracted to a singer who charms rocks, woods, and trees, one who mythology presents as the son of the epic Muse. While the early references, *Ad Patrem*, the *Sixth Elegy*, *Seventh Prolusion*, and the companion poems, invoke Orpheus as model for the aspiring and inspired poet, and "L'Allegro" offers the wish-fulfilling vision of him heaving his head from an Elysian slumber to hear music that would "quite set free" Eurydice, the depiction of Orpheus in the later references is far from placid. *Lycidas* and *Paradise Lost* evoke the violence associated with his death. Those visions are terrifying ones of abandonment. As Orpheus is rent apart, even maternal protection is rendered utterly powerless. "What could the Muse herself that *Orpheus* bore, / The Muse herself for her enchanting son" (*Lycidas*, 58 – 59); "... nor could the Muse defend / Her Son" (*PL*, VII. 37 – 38). Despite all of Milton's assertions of the redemptive power of song, he returns to this haunting image of failure: twice Milton dwells on the inability of poetry to save the poet. If in the elegy the "gory visage" still sings an immortal song as it floats downstream, in the epic Milton drowns the song with the singer: "till the savage clamor drown'd / Both Harp and Voice" (VII. 36 – 37). Joining our hymn to the music of the spheres may enable us to share in Christ's salvation, but Orpheus' song cannot raise the dead. He only "half regains" Eurydice. Of course, Milton attempts to distinguish his song – the hymn – from the one drowned by barbarous dissonance. His Muse is heavenly and would presumably protect him. But Milton's attraction to Orpheus is too powerful and pervasive, the violence too vivid, to be so easily explained away.[73]

Milton expresses hesitation about song elsewhere. The hymn of praise sung by Adam and Eve and the angel choir is contrasted to the devils' song in hell.

> Others more mild,
> Retreated in a silent valley, sing
> With notes Angelical to many a Harp
> Thir own Heroic deed and hapless fall
> By doom of Battle; and complain that Fate
> Free Virtue should enthrall to Force or Chance.

Thir Song was partial, but the harmony
(What could it less when Spirits immortal sing?)
Suspended Hell, and took with ravishment
The thronging audience. (II. 546–55)

The devils' song charms the senses as the song of Circe charms her captives to their ruin in *Comus*. While the angels sing of their Maker's work, the devils sing of their own heroic deeds; they sing, not of birth, but of injury; not of providence, but of chance. Dennis Burden has shown that Milton counterpoints what is essentially Satan's epic – based on the musings of the philosophers of hell on ''Fixt Fate, Free will, Foreknowledge absolute'' (II. 560) – with Milton's epic, which finds its way out of that ''wand'ring maze'' into the providential design.[74] Nevertheless, Milton does not make light of the infernal song; an audience is ravished, hell is suspended. A contest does take place: not just mythically, between creation and chaos and in Heaven's War; not just theoretically, between the philosophers of hell and Milton the theologian; but musically, between choirs. The devils' song surfaces throughout the epic, and the music of the spheres joined to the angel choir and Milton's hymn must silence this infernal charm, lest its dissonance drown the heavenly close forever.

With an undefended Orpheus strewn across Milton's poetic landscape, we cannot claim that he comes to rest securely in the redemptive power of song. It has been remarked that Milton could not write successfully about the death of his God. While he could celebrate his birth in hymn, he could only write the preludium to *The Passion*, and broke off at the hymn itself. The closest Milton does come to depicting the Passion is the dismemberment of Orpheus; in the figure of Orpheus, Milton offers us a singing Christ. When we accept Milton's premise of the prophetic, redemptive activity of the poet, we are led, inevitably, to the figure of a savior-poet, a poet who can raise the dead and create the universe with song. With Orpheus thus understood, his dismemberment is all the more terrible. Milton may approach the Christian myth obliquely, but he is not avoiding the Passion. He contemplates it in the most vivid manner. The vision is not of the simple resurrection Michael lays out before Adam at the end of the poem. Rather, all of the tensions – of injury and recreation, of redemption and defeat – adhere in that far more Miltonic image. Orpheus is rent, but he keeps singing; he sings, but the song is drowned. And it is Milton's choice of Orpheus that creates the final brilliant tension. In his use of the pagan figure, whose revelation is necessarily incomplete, he preserves the hope of a better singer, ''one greater man'' whose song will not die.

4

"YET ONCE MORE": RE-CREATION, REPETITION, AND RETURN

> To banish for ever into a locall hell, whether in the aire or in the center, or in that uttermost and bottomlesse gulph of *Chaos*, deeper from holy blisse then the worlds diameter multiply'd, they thought not a punishing so proper and proportionat for God to inflict, as to punish sinne with sinne.
>
> Milton, *The Doctrine and Discipline of Divorce*

THE TWO FALLS

In calling attention to the hymnic character of *Paradise Lost*, I do not mean to deny that it is a narrative poem, but I have been willing to hammer the point about its generic affinity with hymns for a vital reason. In this poem of many choices, Milton offers two vastly different models for repetition; the *ritual* function that we find in "ceaseless praise" is only one. As we have seen, such repetition signals both the renewal of human memory – to acknowledge contingency is to defeat the chaos of presumption – and the renewal of divine initiative – to praise the creation is ritually to reenact it. Such repeatings are the touchstones of a theodicy in which to remember is to redeem and to be redeemed. But there would be no project of theodicy at all if commemoration were the only mode of repetition driving the poem. Milton would not have to set out to justify his Deity, for a continual hymn of praise would vindicate him; nor would he need to justify loss, for praise suggests reparation: "a grateful mind / By owing owes not" (IV. 55–56). For all of the efforts to praise elaborated in the last chapter, the successful hymn of praise may best be understood as the *goal* of the poem, the sabbath where it would come to rest in silence. For *Paradise Lost* is not only a psalter; the anything-but-silent *narrative* that is also *Paradise Lost* suggests a lapse of memory, a failure in ritual piety, and a loss that begs reparation.

91

Critics have addressed the relation of narrative to loss in various ways. In Edward Said's reading, not only the structure of Milton's narrative, but the very existence of the poem is indebted to loss. If a song of praise commemorates creation, narrative essentially commemorates loss.

> Milton's theme is loss, or absence, and his whole poem represents and commemorates the loss at the most literal level. Thus Milton's anthropology is based on the very writing of his poem, for only because man has lost does he write about it, must he write about it, can he only write about it.[1]

According to Ricoeur, all myths of loss are inevitably shaped into the form of narrative, and this narrative form, he believes, inheres in the very structure of loss.

> The myth [of the origin and end of evil] is a tissue of events and is found nowhere except in the plastic form of narration.... The concrete universality conferred upon human experience by means of archetypal personages, the tension of an ideal history oriented from a Beginning toward an End, and finally the transition from an essential nature to an alienated history; these ... are three aspects of one and the same dramatic structure. Hence, the narrative form is neither secondary nor accidental, but primitive and essential.[2]

There are, however, not one, but two myths of the fall in *Paradise Lost*; the poem elaborates two different narratives of loss. Satan's fall is a myth of loss leading only to continual renunciation and relapse; Adam's fall is a myth of loss leading to repentance and recovery. The conflict between chaos and creation is also articulated in terms of these separate falls, a fall that issues in an unrelieved curse of "death and woe" – a perpetual chaos – and a fortunate one, that issues in re-creation. The distinction between these two narratives is graphically illustrated by their respective rituals. While the aubade of Adam and Eve that celebrates creation effects a re-creation, Satan performs an infernal worship service: forever reaching for the apple in hell that turns to ashes, he repeats the same futile gesture to the same fruitless conclusion.

The myth of the fortunate fall can be seen as a tale of delayed gratification: our fallen life becomes a temporary unpleasure when it is seen in the context of the long if arduous road to final redemption. Like Freud's pleasure principle, *felix culpa* presupposes the existence of a dominant drive toward fulfillment. But Milton's impulse to go "beyond" the Christian myth of the fall is analogous to Freud's choice to go "beyond the pleasure principle."[3] When Milton chooses to narrate the myth of that *second* fall, he narrates a new logic in which pain is no temporary state on the road to pleasure. He moves beyond that pleasure principle to describe a Satanic principle. Satan does not turn his back, like Donne, to receive corrections, nor does he endure goads and checks, as Dante imagines, that are designed to inspire and purge. Rather, in the story of Satan, Milton places the myth of a fatal fall alongside the myth of the fortunate one, and there is, I hope to show, much to be learned by their sheer juxtaposition: the juxtaposition of pathological, compulsive repetition with ritual, willed repetition. Like the Burghers, Satan remembers nothing and learns nothing.

When Freud first encountered the compulsion to repeat, he felt that for the first time his pleasure principle could not suffice as an explanatory mechanism. Observing the steps that Freud takes toward his new principle, the principle "beyond",[4] Ricoeur notes that Freud might have accommodated even the repetitious inducement of pain to the pleasure principle in several ways. First, unpleasure could have been seen as a temporary condition to be tolerated in the service of future pleasure. But unpleasant repetitions do not issue in delayed gratification – only in further repetitions of pain. Then again, what is unpleasurable in one stage of development may have been pleasurable in another phase of psychic organization. But once a new stage is consolidated, unpleasure can no longer be understood as a vestige.[5] And so Freud put aside these possible solutions, choosing the radical path of a new principle, "the operation of tendencies ... more primitive than the pleasure principle and independent of it."[6] "What follows," Freud tells us, "is speculation," and what follows is Freud's elaboration of the death instinct. Henceforth, his battleground will seem to shift to Eros and Thanatos. Derrida has complicated this account, demonstrating that despite all his "numerous marching orders and steps," Freud does not go beyond the pleasure principle in his work of that title; rather, he confirms its authority, playing his own *fort-da* game with that "something" beyond.[7] Then, too, Laplanche has demonstrated a more subtle relation between Eros and Thanatos; like Milton's good and evil, they are not only conflicting, but mutually constituting.[8] Ricoeur would also modify any simplistic dualism:

Instead of being a clear delimitation of two domains, the dualism of Eros and Thanatos appears as a dramatic *overlapping of roles*. In a sense, everything is death, since self-preservation is the circuitous path on which each living substance pursues its own death. In another sense, everything is life, since narcissism itself is a figure of Eros.[9]

It is with this caution that I will delineate a distinction between
the myth of Adam and the myth of Satan, between virtually a life
principle and a death instinct in *Paradise Lost*. But I will conclude
that the distinction between those two principles may not be so neat,
for the myths of the fatal fall and the fortunate fall may be, like the
death and life instincts, and like chaos and creation, as mutually
constituting as they are contradictory. Furthermore, while I will
begin by drawing a very broad distinction between compulsive
repetition and ritual repetition, it is with the caveat that "purely
defensive or purely nondefensive behavior are fictions."[10]

THE SATANIC WILL

The relation of ritual repetition to time is inherently contradictory:
on the one hand, ritual acknowledges the passing of time; to
"remember" an event is to assume that it has occurred in the past
and can only be recovered imaginatively. On the other hand, the
function of ritual is to escape time, to offer its participants entry
into a separated time where event and commemoration are one.
Compulsive repetition is predicated on a different relation to time.
Such repetition reflects an attempt to "get even" for an insult or
affront to the psychic apparatus, but because the continual passing
of time renders the effort to "get even" or re-do an injury impossible,
the compulsive repeater would stop time, as Miss Havisham stopped
her clocks in *Great Expectations*. Satan would not only avenge himself
against his accusor, but against time itself, and he depicts his fall
not as any wound, but specifically, as a *change*.

> how chang'd
> From him, who in the happy Realms of Light
> Cloth'd with transcendent brightness didst outshine
> Myriads though bright: (I. 84–87)

And that change immediately inspires him to refuse any further
change.

> yet not for those,
> nor what the Potent Victor in his rage
> Can else inflict, do I repent or change,
> Though chang'd in outward luster; (I. 94–97)

The distinction he grasps for here, between outward and inward
change, is obviously specious; he knows, as we know, that the inner
reflects the outer, and amidst his verbal flailing between "change"
and "no change," the simple truth emerges that he *has* changed

94

and that he now stubbornly wills that change to be irrevocable. Indeed, his conjunction might well be more forcefully causal: Satan does not seize upon his resolve "though" changed in outward luster, but "because" of that diminishment. He will fix the will or "harden the heart" toward a single purpose. It is fixity, a "fixt mind / And high disdain," that emerges from the "sense of injur'd merit" he cannot recover (I. 98 – 99).

Having suffered loss, Satan grasps for that which can brook no loss. If heaven cannot be his eternally, then at least hate can be immortal. In his frustration that he cannot recapture the past, to un-do and re-do it, he tries to seize control of change itself.

> What though the field be lost:
> All is not lost; the unconquerable Will,
> And study of revenge, immortal hate,
> And courage never to submit or yield:
> And what is else not to be overcome? (I. 105 – 09)

These words are fraught with telling contradictions. "*Having lost*, I refuse to lose; *having been forced to yield*, I refuse to yield." And that last odd question, "what is else not to be overcome?" seductively suggests conflicting meanings. On the one hand, it suggests the tautology, "my will never to be overcome will never be overcome"; on the other, self-justification: "I must embrace revenge and hate for only they are of lasting consequence." But there is a more desperate underside to the sentiment: "We have been so thoroughly defeated that nothing is left us – 'what is else?' – but defiance itself." The ostensibly heroic lines want to collapse into a plaintive "What have we left?" And the confusion we note here spills over into their sequel: "That Glory never shall his wrath or might / Extort from me" (I. 110 – 11). What glory? The glory of revenge and hate, the glory of resolve itself? Is there a "glory" left for Satan that has not been "extorted" already? Satan answers that question himself, deflating his own posturing less than thirty lines later: all glory is "extinct" (I. 141). The contradictions in these lines stem from a fundamental one: Satan's will to be unconquerable is born of the essential impotence of his will.

Nietzsche speaks of this impotence of the will in the face of time as its prison.

Willing liberates; but what is it that puts even the liberator himself in fetters? "It was" – that is the name of the will's gnashing of teeth and most secret melancholy. Powerless against what has been done, he is an angry spectator of all that is past. The will cannot will backwards; and that he cannot break time and time's covetousness, that is the will's loneliest melancholy.[11]

It is a desperate assertion of mastery where there can be none that drives Satan to *choose* that hell of a bound will rather than suffer it. Satan's resolve of an unchanging mind and his appropriation of hell can now be seen as analogous efforts: to convert defeat into a choice. The victim of time and place would rule both time and place.

> Hail horrors, hail
> Infernal world, and thou profoundest Hell
> Receive thy new Possessor: One who brings
> A mind not to be chang'd by Place or Time.
>
> (I. 250–53)

Nietzsche's words could be Satan's manifesto: "To recreate all 'it was' into a 'thus I willed it' – that alone I should call redemption." Like Hamlet, Satan could be bounded in a nutshell and count himself the king of infinite space – "the mind is its own place, and in itself / Can make a Heav'n of Hell" (I. 254–55) – were it not that he has bad dreams – "which way I fly is Hell, myself am Hell" (IV. 75).

Because of the irreversibility of the flow of time, the effort to re-do the past erupts in repetitions and substitutions. To avenge themselves on God, the fallen angels would repeat their fall in man. They would "drive as we were driven" (II. 366). Nietzsche speaks of revenge as the logical consequence of time's restraint.

what means does the will devise for himself to get rid of his melancholy and to mock his dungeon? Alas, every prisoner becomes a fool; and the imprisoned will redeems himself foolishly. That time does not run backwards, that is his wrath; "that which was" is the name of the stone he cannot move. And so he moves stones out of wrath and displeasure, and he wreaks revenge on whatever does not feel wrath and displeasure as he does. Thus the will, the liberator, took to hurting; and on all who can suffer he wreaks revenge for his inability to go backwards. This, indeed this alone, is what *revenge* is: the will's ill will against time and its "it was."[12]

Re-inflicting his injury on others, Satan finds that it only redounds upon himself, and he falls forever. "Revenge, at first though sweet, / Bitter ere long back on itself recoils" (IX. 171–72). Such repetitions only lock him in his injury, precluding any genuine change, precluding, that is, innovation. Ironically, Satan's drive for fixity is fulfilled in this iterative sense. Vengeful repetition is linked to fixity in another sense: born of a sense of impotence, it confirms the feeling of paralysis of the will – for repetitions which are derived from injury are not so much willed, as they are compelled.

When Freud linked the need to master an injury to the compulsive nature of repetition,[13] he observed that a child at play could derive no obvious pleasure from reenacting the disappearance of his mother – hiding and recovering a spool in the *fort-da* game – except that now the child could control the absence and presence of the object. The formal expression of this attempted mastery, the game, has important implications. The *fort-da* game is not only motivated by the child's inability to control his mother's leave-takings; the very fact of the game itself confirms his ineffectuality.[14] The real object of his frustration is never mastered. The mother's will is never subject to the child's. The child's domain, like Satan's hell, is no domain at all, and his substitutive and repetitive efforts to master, like Satan's, are only the semblance of control. Pande-monium is just such a play-domain. While it is erected in an effort to replace what is lost – with the roof of that "fabric huge" mirroring the floor of heaven, its "Starry Lamps and blazing Cressets ... yielded light / As from a sky" (I. 728 – 30) – the size similes that conclude Book I mock that effort, reducing the capital to a beehive. The game-world circumscribing the infernal will is underscored again in the account of the pursuits of the devils. Their philosophy, poetry, and war exercises are described, as we might expect, as means to "entertain / The irksome hours" (IV. 526 – 27), that is, as play, not as solutions. Even that most serious business of the temptation and fall of man, where the real-life consequence is death, is enveloped by an aura of childsplay. Satan cannot heave his head from off the fiery flood without the "will / And high per-mission" (I. 211 – 12) of his Father; and with his reiterated crime only redounding upon his own head, the redemption of man is implicit from the very beginning. The essential futility of re-doing by repeating is expressed most forcefully in that terrible game.

The quality that emerges most consistently in the portrayal of Satanic mastery, then, is that it is false.

> Nor hope to be myself less miserable
> By what I seek, but others to make such
> As I, though thereby worse to me redound:
>
> (IX. 126 – 28)

The attempt to master past injuries by seeking revenge is grounded both in the sense that there is nothing to lose and that nothing could really be gained. Even amidst Satan's rallying efforts and contrivance of revenge plots during the debate in hell, the idea of achieving reparation, if entertained, is never seriously anticipated. We can detect little confidence in Satan's first proposal that the injured parties seek revenge.

> Thither let us tend
> From off the tossing of these fiery waves,
> There rest, if any rest can harbor there,
> And reassembling our afflicted Powers,
> Consult how we may henceforth most offend
> Our Enemy, our own loss how repair,
> How overcome this dire Calamity,
> What reinforcement we may gain from Hope,
> If not what resolution from despair. (I. 183–91)

That repair/despair rhyme is suggestive. The effort to repair through repeating is born of despair, and such an attempt at reparation can only conclude in despair. The little optimism that begins this passage soon dissipates, until by the last line no "overcoming" is imaginable; we are left only with resolve. Even when Satan triumphantly proclaims that he leaves hell to seek deliverance, at the same time, he adjures the devils to search for a way to render hell more tolerable (II. 456–66). Beelzebub seems to contradict Satan's realism, venturing the most hopeful lines uttered during the debate in hell. He envisions no less than the restoration of heaven's light to those who tempt man, and he speaks explicitly of the possibility of healing their injury. Still, this optimism is hedged with tentativeness, and like Satan's speeches, the "perhapses" and "we may chances" utterly collapse into the alternative vision – "or else" – and a fantasy of "some mild zone" ensues.

> Great things resolv'd, which from the lowest deep
> Will once more lift us up, in spite of Fate,
> Nearer our ancient Seat; perhaps in view
> Of those bright confines, whence with neighboring Arms
> And opportune excursion we may chance
> Re-enter Heav'n; or else in some mild Zone
> Dwell not unvisited of Heav'n's fair Light
> Secure, ...
> ... the soft delicious Air,
> To heal the scar of these corrosive Fires
> Shall breathe her balm. (II. 392–402)

Beelzebub's shaky hope stands on even shakier ground, for his plan for this reparation – indeed, the entire argument to seduce man – is based wholly on the opposite conviction, that heaven is impenetrable: its "high walls fear no assault or Siege, / Or ambush from the Deep" (II. 343–44). Moloch's imagined victories (turning "our Tortures into horrid Arms / Against the Torturer") also fade, like Satan's strained optimism, into his admission of complete ineffectuality. The devils' power may be sufficient to "disturb his Heaven", but then again, it may only "Alarm, / Though inaccessible, his fatal Throne" (II. 103–4). His apologetic conclusion – "Which if not Victory is yet Revenge" – admits that the two are not at all synonymous.

The only significant difference between the plans of the rough-hewn Moloch and Satan's more wily plot is substitution. Moloch would storm heaven again; Satan would also try again, on earth. Their common advocacy of desperate repetition far outweighs that difference. With his look of "desperate revenge," Moloch not only voices, he embodies the logic of Satanic repetition. The consequence Moloch imagines, falling again, is precisely the one Satan knows he will suffer for his "reiterated crimes" (I. 214). In this sense, the infernal debate has already closed with its first, not its last, speaker. The fact that there is no substantive change from Moloch's to Satan's positions about how to rectify their plight – to "match torment with torment" is "to drive as we were driven" – reflects the characteristic stasis of revenge: for all their talk, they cannot move forward. Because revenge, by its very character, never achieves satisfaction, the effort to turn "it was" into "thus I willed it" through substitutions and repeatings can find "no end, in wand'ring mazes lost" (II. 561).

Such repetitions of injury issue in death, or, more accurately, in the death-in-life that denies even an end to life's torments: it is not only as liminal figures, but as perpetual victims who perpetually victimize, that the devils become "neither living nor dead from one aspect and both living and dead from another."[15] Satan is "to Death devote" (IX. 901). He repeats his injury with the hope, not just of expelling mankind, but with the more comprehensive aim of wasting the whole creation. As we have seen, the fallen angels talk nervously of the possibility of being completely annihilated and Satan forms a natural alliance with the uncreated chaos. But to understand fully the relation between death and Satanic repetition, we must turn to the allegory of Sin and Death. Milton was willing to take this generic adventure, risk incurring the future wrath of a Samuel Johnson – "This unskillful allegory appears to me one of the greatest faults of the poem"[16] – because only in allegory could the fundamental logic of compulsive repetition be fully addressed. Allegorical characters are projections of the self, and Satan's in-cestuous self-reproduction graphically illustrates that the issue of such repetition is not a new creation, but Death.[17]

Doubling is the spatial form of temporal repetition, and its source, according to both Freud and Otto Rank, is narcissism.[18] In Satan's refusal to confront a genuine Other – for such an Other would be an insult to the grandeur of the all-encompassing Self – he reproduces only projections of the Self. Like all regressive tendencies, narcissism has as its goal "the attempt to return to a state in which subject and object did not yet exist, to a time before that division occurred out of which the ego sprang,"[19] to a time when Self and Other were combined in an internal love union. Thus, we might expect narcissism ultimately to lead back to the womb. But Freud would see this return as a regression to a state even earlier – the state of non-being prior to birth. This becomes the ultimate return; for Freud, all compulsive repetitions, doubling included, are really disguised attempts to restore the original state of non-being. As the classical myth tells it, narcissism leads to death. While Freud tries to ground this theory of the death instinct organically in *Beyond the Pleasure Principle*, he might well have written the allegory of Sin and Death instead.

Satan's narcissism is most powerfully in evidence in his refusal to acknowledge the Other, his Creator. His claim to be self-begotten, his resistance to the Son, all bespeak a towering self-love. He responds to the elevation of the Son with more than denial: he responds by reproducing himself in his own image, conceiving Sin. With Sin his "perfect image," "likest to [him] in shape and count'nance bright" (II. 756), Satan's love for Sin is self-love. The doubling continues, until the repetitions issue in Death, but again, not a final death, for the deadly offspring of Sin and Death are "hourly conceiv'd / And hourly born" (II. 796–97). What is most painful in that "Sight hateful, sight tormenting" of Adam and Eve "imparadis't in one another's arms" (IV. 505, 506) is the fact that *two* are participating in that embrace. As Rank explains, noting the phenomenon in Oscar Wilde's *Dorian Gray*, narcissism precludes love for another: " 'I wish I could love,' cried Dorian Gray, with a deep note of pathos in his voice. 'But I seem to have lost the passion, and forgotten the desire. *I am too much concentrated on myself* [Rank's emphasis]. My own personality has become a burden to me. I want to escape, to go away, to forget.' "[20] Satan acknowledges that not the least of his pains is his perpetual longing, and the narcissistic origins of that frustration are confirmed when Eve gazes at her fair image in the pool: she too would have "pin'd with vain desire" (IV. 466).

While Milton reserves the classical type scene of narcissism for Eve,[21] she echoes the doubling of Satan and Sin. Had the warning voice not led her away from her watery image to the Other, Eve would have succumbed to doubling.

Re-creation, repetition, and return

> A Shape within the wat'ry gleam appear'd
> Bending to look on me, I started back,
> It started back, but pleas'd I soon return'd,
> Pleas'd it return'd as soon with answering looks
> Of sympathy and love;   (IV. 461–65)

Both Sin and Eve are engendered without mothers. Both are born
– and the detail must have been deliberate – from the left side of
their parent/mate; Milton truncates his line that describes Sin's birth,
allowing the ambiguity about the precise nature of that generation
to echo for several verses before he clarifies that Sin is born from
Satan's head and not from his rib.

> till on the left side op'ning wide,
> Likest to thee in shape and count'nance bright,
> Then shining heav'nly fair, a Goddess arm'd
> Out of thy head I sprung: (II. 755–58)

When Eve does fall, she prophesies that the issue of her loins, like
Sin's, will be "Food for so foul a Monster" (X. 986). Conversely,
Eve's initial renunciation of narcissism is proleptic of her later turn
away from mothering generations and generations "devote" to
death. Eve, who is brought away from her image, taken "where no
shadow stays / Thy coming" (IV. 470–71), (where, that is, no
double forestalls her) will not spawn endless doubles: she will be the
mother of Life, not Death.

Self-love, the love of the double, does not suffice to explain the
whole response to this shadow self; the reaction is far more ambi-
valent. Any notion of an ideal self involves the guilty rejection of
those desires and instincts which do not fit that ideal image. When
these internal anomalies are cast out, they also return externalized
as the double.[22] And so the individual is both attracted and repelled
by this self-image. Satan is so abhorred by his Sin that he cannot,
or will not, recognize it as his own.

> I know thee not, nor ever saw till now
> Sight more detestable than him and thee.   (II. 744–45)

While Satan's inability to recognize Sin and Death may become
comic, that failure also suggests a profound insight into just this self-
loathing. What Satan rejects as most offensive is, of course, his
own mortality, and the double becomes a haunting reminder of that
limitation. Satan sees, not just Death, but *his* death and that is why
he recoils from it in horror.

101

> Whence and what are thou, execrable shape,
> That dar'st, though grim and terrible, advance
> Thy miscreated Front athwart my way
> To yonder Gates? (II. 681–84)

Satan's will to master that which makes him most impotent asserts itself again. That will-to-master coupled with the loathing of the rejected self makes murder of the double his likely goal. But to master death, to kill the double, is to commit suicide. Satan's confrontation with death – "No second stroke intend" (II. 713) – is ultimately a suicide scene. That implication becomes explicit when Death pursues but does not devour his other double, Sin; that too would be suicide, in this case, the end of Death itself.

> Before mine eyes in opposition sits
> Grim *Death* my Son and foe, who sets them on,
> And me his Parent would full soon devour
> For want of other prey, but that he knows
> His end with mine involv'd; and knows that I
> Should prove a bitter Morsel, and his bane,
> Whenever that shall be; (II. 803–09)

Linking narcissism to thanatophobia, Rank points out that for the sufferer, it is not the fear of death, but "the *expectation* of the unavoidable destiny of death [that] is unbearable." Again, he aptly quotes Dorian Gray, " 'I have no terror of Death. It is only *the coming* of death that terrifies me.' "[23]

The normally unconscious thought of the approaching destruction of the self – the most general example of the repression of an unendurable certainty – torments these unfortunates with the conscious idea of their eternal, eternal [*sic*] inability to return, an idea from which release is only possible in death. Thus we have the strange paradox of the suicide who voluntarily seeks death in order to free himself of the intolerable thanatophobia.[24]

If Satan's effort to master death, rather, to master his dread of death, is deferred here in Book II, it is only to be enacted later in the more involuted manner of the temptation and fall. Sin predicts that this aborted battle with Death will be resumed, conducted by "His wrath which one day will destroy ye both" (II. 734). The narrator seconds Sin's comparison of the mock fight between Death and Satan to a final showdown between Satan and Christ.

> so matcht they stood;
> For never but once more was either like
> To meet so great a foe: (II. 720–22)

Doubling proliferates temporally as well as spatially – the doubles
will meet their doubles once more. This "once more," like the "once
more" of "Lycidas," refers to the final battle at Judgment Day. That
allusion suggests that doubling extends beyond Satan and Death:
Satan is also Christ's double. Satan is the rejected self, the rejected
son, who pursues and is pursued until he is killed, while Christ
becomes a glorified suicide. Hebrews tells us that he is incarnated
so that "through death he might destroy him who has the power of
death, that is, the devil, and deliver all those who through fear of
death were subject to lifelong bondage" (2:14b, 15).

ADAMIC RETURN

From its inception, every need "constitutes simultaneously a wish
and a fear": the hope that the wish will be fulfilled and the fear that
it will not.[25] Man's dual responses to immortality – as wish and
fear – have inspired the dual myths of Adam and Satan. While
Satan is, strictly speaking, immortal, his quest for dominion is lost,
and he is unable to escape the defenses of revenge. In Adam, the
same drive to grasp his wish – rather than await it – is also in
evidence. When his impatience denies him that immortality, he
initially responds with the same cyclic effort to master the loss that
Satan does in his encounter with his deadly double: a suicide wish.
Like Satan's will to destruction, Adam's death wish is born of
thanatophobia: "Ay me, that fear [of an endless death] / Comes
thund'ring back with dreadful revolution / On my defenseless head"
(X. 813 – 15). Adam's sense of defenselessness is ironic, armed as
he is with the defensive suicide wish, and doubly ironic in light of
his genuine defense of repentance. Adam speaks in the reflexive
language of redounding and recoiling so familiar from Satan: "all
from mee / Shall with a fierce reflux on mee redound" (X. 738 – 39).
His injury will issue in an endless repetition of further injuries: he
can "increase and multiply" nothing but curses in succeeding ages.
Eve's contemplation of suicide also betrays the same impulse that
governs Satan's abortive efforts to take control: she too would bring
the dreaded future down upon herself.

> Why stand we longer shivering under fears,
> That show no end but Death, and have the power,
> Of many ways to die the shortest choosing,
> Destruction with destruction to destroy.
>
> (X. 1003 – 06)

Eve's version of Satan's resolve is willing sterility and death.But so long as they are suicidal, Eve and Adam cannot move beyond the thinking that inspired their fall – the will to master death is equivalent to the will to master immortality.

It is this inauthentic grasping of the future that first stirs Adam to reject the trap of Satanic repetition. He knows that mastering his curse is futile, that the future would not be thus forestalled. "Death / So snatcht will not exempt us from the pain / We are by doom to pay" (X. 1024–26). The capacity that enables the unfallen Adam to imagine death without any experience of it – "whatev'r Death is" – now allows the fallen Adam to imagine something *other* than death, something other than the state he now experiences. He refuses the option to repeat what he already knows, electing not to avenge himself by taking control of the inevitable. In fact, he leaves behind the very notion of "inevitable." Adam takes up the task enjoined him at his birth: to be the creator of something new. His example teaches that the compelled repeater is fundamentally afflicted with a dire lack of imagination. Satan can only conceive of doing what has been done. Repentance is innovative; to refuse to repeat consti-tutes a genuine act of the will. Indeed this is Augustine's under-standing of the will: " '*initium ut esset homo creatus est*,' man's capacity for beginning because he himself is a beginning."[26]

When he is in despair, Adam speaks of novelty as an aberration, even if it does enable generation.

> O why did God,
> Creator wise, that peopl'd highest Heav'n
> With Spirits Masculine, create at last
> This novelty on Earth, this fair defect
> Of nature, and fill the World at once
> With Men as Angels without Feminine,
> Or find some other way to generate
> Mankind? (X. 888–95)

Nonetheless, Adam's originality is given best expression generatively, in his children. Unlike Satan's progeny, they are not merely reproductions of death, the increase and multiplication of the curse. They are new life, born of female novelty, and they issue in that new form, the radically innovative God-man, who will gently waft us "to immortal Life" (XII. 435).

Milton tells us that "Prevenient Grace descending had remov'd / The stony from thir hearts, and made new flesh / Regenerate grow instead" (XI. 3–5). But he also supplements his doctrine on grace with an insightful portrait of the psychology of repentance. One of the projects of psychoanalysis is to make the patient feel that he is an actor, *willing* those acts which he had previously felt to be automatic and autonomous. This process requires the recognition that the conflicts and defenses of the psyche are his own; as Hans Loewald describes this awareness, that the dream *I had* was *my* dream.[27] This process of recognition – making available to consciousness what had previously been the province of the unconscious – becomes, then, the prerequisite for a new organizing activity. Only with recognition can we make what was once "compelled" properly "willed." While such recognition invites the language of psychoanalysis – we speak of "making conscious," or "ego organization" – there is a term in religious parlance for this same coming to awareness: confession. Confession also involves the activity of acknowledging as *one's own*, and in the psychology that is religion, confession enables the turn to a new content, laying open the possibility for a genuine act of willing: willing away from error. In this sense, confession becomes the means to reverse the spiral downward; it holds that place in Augustine and in Dante, as it does in Milton. It enables the recognition of repetition *as* repetition, and that re-cognition allows a new content. The patristic tripartite structure of penance – confession, contrition, and satisfaction – reflects this psychology, for in it, *acknowledgment* is both distinct from, and prior to, contrition and reparation.[28]

Milton's scene of the Curse in the Garden is characterized by inadequate confession. Both Adam and Eve refuse to take responsibility for their acts; both deny that they are actors. Eve only pretends to "confessing soon" as she transfers the fault to Satan: "The Serpent me beguil'd and I did eat" (X. 162). But Eve cannot disown this nightmare. It was not planted by a toad at her ear. Adam follows suit, blaming his deed on the Creator's bad creation instead: "This Woman whom thou mad'st to be my help, / And gav'st me as thy perfet gift, ... / Shee gave me of the Tree, and I did eat" (X. 137 – 38, 143). Adam sounds just like the Satan who veers away from acknowledging his fault only to blame "Heav'n's free Love dealt equally to all" (IV. 68). Only when Adam and Eve replace their false confession by a true one – when, that is, they acknowledge their deed as theirs – do they enable repetition with a difference. At that moment, they betray a subtle distinction between compelled repetition and willed return, for it is as a *return* to the "place of judgment" in order to be judged again, but differently, that their "innovation" from the Satanic pattern is cast.

>   both have sinn'd, but thou
> Against God only, I against God and thee,
> And to the place of judgment will return,
> There with my cries importune Heaven, that all
> The sentence from thy head remov'd may light
> On me, sole cause to thee of all this woe,
> Mee mee only just object of his ire.
>
>   (X. 930–36)

Eve is overzealous here, owning more fault than is her due, and without a warning voice, she is susceptible to lapsing into narcissism again, the narcissism – "me, sole ... mee mee only" – of self-pity. Instead, her "fault acknowledg'd" inspires Adam to reclaim his share.

>   her lowly plight,
> Immovable till peace obtain'd from fault
> Acknowledg'd and deplor'd, in *Adam* wrought
> Commiseration;   (X. 937–40)

Memory plays a key role in their movement toward repentance. Adam "Remember[s] with what mild / And gracious temper" his judgment was delivered, and that enables him to repair to the place of judgment where he will proceed to repair his injury. Freud's dictum in "Remembering, Repeating, and Working-Through" is that what a patient cannot remember he acts out.

He reproduces it not as a memory but as an action; he *repeats* it, without, of course, knowing that he is repeating it. For instance, the patient does not say that he remembers that he used to be defiant and critical towards his parents' authority; instead he behaves that way to the doctor.[29]

Ricoeur stresses the point, citing this relation of memory to acting out as the decisive insight that led Freud beyond the pleasure principle. Compulsive repetition is "the tendency of the patient to repeat the repressed material as a contemporary experience instead of remembering it as a past memory."[30] Presumably the converse is true; what is available to memory need not be acted out. Appropriating the past *as past* relieves the pressure to repeat compulsively. Innovation is predicated on the pastness of the past.

Loewald looks at the process in detail, and he arrives at categories that are not unlike my own "Satanic repetition" and "Adamic return." His distinction is between passive and active forms of repetition which are, in turn, the result of either passive or conscious remembering. "Conscious recollection, in the sense in which in analysis we attempt to have the patient substitute it for reproductive [elsewhere termed passive] repeating, would be an act of re-creating, the moment of generating new organization from something old."[31] Furthermore, he links such active remembering to recognition, to the kind of awareness that Adam and Eve achieve in order to repent. "To acknowledge, recognize, understand one's unconscious as one's own means to move from a position of passivity in relation to it to a position where active care of it becomes possible."[32] Infernal psychology is characterized by passivity. Such notions as "fate," "destiny," and "fortune" are not just trying to explain the order of things by *any* principle other than providence; they are the terminology of a passive psychology. He who suffers change rather than creates it speaks of "destiny"; he who compulsively repeats rather than actively wills speaks of "fate." Satan's memory affords no relief from this fated pattern. What was must be: to recall an injury is only to reproduce it. His memories are no active recognition of his fault; they afford passive capitulation to his pain. Satan's memories do not appropriate the past as past, rather, they become prophecies of his future.

> Now conscience wakes despair
> That slumber'd, wakes the bitter memory
> Of what he was, what is, and what must be
> Worse; of worse deeds worse sufferings must ensue.
> (IV. 23 – 26)

Satan hates beams that only remind him of his paralysis of the will: "to thee I call, ... O Sun, to tell thee how I hate thy beams / That bring to my remembrance from what state / I fell" (IV. 35 – 39). The sun inspires memory of his loss, but no ritual recompense, not in mourning – which would place the loss in the past – and certainly not in praise. In his scheme, such praise would only issue in a "worse relapse, / And heavier fall" (IV. 100 – 01). But there is an alternative to this pathological repetition, and another address to the sun marks that alternative. As we have seen, that same sun inspires praise in Adam and Eve, invites them to partake of a ritual shared by all of creation, and insures future re-creations. The sun stirs "prompt eloquence" (V. 149) in them instead of rancor, and the ritual dispels any pain lingering from the temptation dream.

There is a third address to the sun. While Milton has neatly bifurcated the compulsive and ritual responses to loss in Satan and Adam's addresses, he mixes those responses, confronting the full complexity of their interrelation in his own invocation to light.[33] First, he evokes the creation. The light, whether eternal or coeternal, is the light that "with a Mantle didst invest / The rising world of waters dark and deep, / Won from the void and formless infinite" (III. 10–12). There is another evocation of Genesis in the catalogue of morning and evening, the seasons, herbs, flocks, and "human face divine." While those beautiful lines could sound like a hymn of praise, they become instead a lament, for the light is denied him. Milton cannot sing the hymn of praise when he is denied the creation. In the Psalms, the dead cannot offer praise or give thanks:

> Do the shades rise up to praise thee?
> Is thy steadfast love declared in the grave, ...
> Are thy wonders known in the darkness,
> or thy saving help in the land of forgetfulness?
>
> (Ps. 88:10–12)

As Milton speaks of loss, the language of repetition grows insistent. He begins his address by recounting that he has ventured "down / The dark descent" (III. 19–20) but now he "revisit[s]" the light. He proceeds to rehearse that nightly he visits Muses' haunt. He "revisits" the sun, but it "revisit'st not" his eyes, "that roll in vain / To find thy piercing ray, and find no dawn" (III. 23–24). While the seasons "return," "not to me returns / Day" (III. 41–42). But he neither hates the sun for failing to revisit him, nor does he respond defensively to that absence, willing an eternal eclipse. Rather, the address to the sun becomes a very catalogue of loss, a ritual expression of mourning. It is a complex response, for Milton simultaneously "remembers" his most cherished wish, the creation, and remembers that it is lost to him. He does not opt for the one memory to the exclusion of the other. Rather, the invocation expresses the interdependence of his greatest wish and deepest fear. In the invocation, Milton cries out for vision, but "[w]ho is to say whether the initial crying out of need is crying out against the need as threat or a cry for help or both?"[34]

What, we must ask, enables Milton to turn from Satan's logic? What prevents his imagining an endless revisiting, haunting his loss nightly in haunting the Muses' grove? We could speak of the completion of mourning, of the internalization of the absent object that finally frees one from the perpetual feeling of loss. Milton's light shines inward now, just as Adam's lost paradise becomes a "paradise within thee, happier far" (XII. 587).

>   ever-during dark
> Surrounds me, from the cheerful ways of men
> Cut off, and for the Book of knowledge fair

Presented with a Universal blanc
Of Nature's works to me expung'd and ras'd,
And wisdom at one entrance quite shut out.
So much the rather thou Celestial Light
Shine inward   (III. 45–52)

But that triumphant conclusion is more the expression than the
explanation of Milton's non-Satanic response to loss. Adamic ritual
offers a key. When Ricoeur analyzes the compulsion to repeat, he
veers in a different direction from Freud's death instinct. What
interests the philosopher about the *fort-da* example, as we might
expect, is the *symbolic* nature of that repetition. He writes that
"symbolism and play also repeat unpleasure, not compulsively,
but by creating symbolism out of absence."[35] If that symbolic
expression of repetition were to be codified into a form, enacted by
a group, and supported by a cultural institution, it would be not a
pathological response to change, but a ritual one.

Milton's lament is not a private occasion, not even the pseudo-
private one of a soliloquy. It is cast in the most formal and public
of modes, the epic invocation. Milton is able to confront his pain
fully *because* of that public forum, not despite it. He jeers about his
blindness in his correspondence to Salmasius; he weeps here,
organizing that grief within the framework of a noble literary tradition. In the context of that "epic ritual," Milton is able to re-create,
just as the ritual hymn ensured Adam and Eve's redemption and
affirmed the cosmic creation.

Satan's memory is more selective. He recalls his defeat but forgets
his making, "Forgetful what from him [he] still receiv'd" (IV. 54).
Augustine also speaks of a selective memory, but one that opts for
the opposite choice, to forget pain and remember happiness. He gives
his discussion of memory prominence of place, for it concludes his
description of the city of God.

[I]n the everlasting City, there will remain in each and all of us an inalienable
freedom of the will, emancipating us from every evil and filling us with every
good, rejoicing in the inexhaustible beatitude of everlasting happiness,
unclouded by the memory of any sin or of sanction suffered, yet with no
forgetfulness of our redemption nor any loss of gratitude for our
Redeemer.[36]

He proceeds to elaborate on this notion of selective memory. In one of
the more striking coincidences of intellectual history, Augustine arrives at a conclusion about memory very like Freud's, and he does so
by using a familiar example. His metaphor of physical pain suffered

by patients and observed by physicians looks toward Freud's analysis of victims of "traumatic neurosis."

> The memory of our previous miseries will be a matter of purely mental contemplation, with no renewal of any feelings connected with these experiences – much as learned doctors know by science many of those bodily maladies which, by suffering, they have no sensible experience.[37]

Distinguishing between "notional" and "experiential" understanding enables Augustine to consign pain to the province of thought. In Freudian terms, it will be *remembered* rather than reenacted. "It is one thing to be a philosopher, learning by ethical analysis the nature of each and every vice, and another to be a scoundrel, learning his lessons from a dissolute life."[38] Even the moral judgment implicit here is not unfamiliar to psychoanalysis. At the risk of violating the law of objectivity in the discipline, Loewald suggests that the analyst values and seeks to instill the value of recognition that enables re-creation.[39] Psychoanalysts would make philosophers of us all.

The likeness ends here. While Freud's reflections on traumatic neurosis lead him to compulsive repetition and the death instinct, Augustine's metaphor of pain leads him in the opposite direction, to the easing of sensible pain and to everlasting life. He slides gracefully from his discourse on memory to praise. The saints will remember the idea of pain, "For, if they had no kind of memory of past miseries, how could the Psalmist have said: 'The mercies of the Lord they will sing for ever'?"[40] And from praise he turns to ritual, to the final sabbath. "On that day we shall rest and see, see and love, love and praise – for this is to be the end without the end of all our living, that Kingdom without end, the real goal of our present life."[41] In such an understanding of everlasting life – for Kierkegaard the only true repetition is eternity – time does not imprison the will and events of the past are not impossible to recover. Time is only an illusion, not a tormentor. This final rest is not possible for a Satan. Peace and rest can never dwell in a hell of endless revenge. In a demonic parody of the exodus, Satan's first movement is from the burning lake to the "dry land." But the land burns too; Satan has moved from one injury to the next: "Such resting found the sole / Of unblest feet" (I. 237–38). As Milton's epic begins with a false, demonic sabbath, it concludes with the hope of a genuine sabbath, with the cautious steps of our first parents seeking a "place of rest." It is a charged phrase, for even as it raised the specter of Satanic repetition, it alludes to the ritual repetition of creation – and that commemoration of *the* beginning may best express their new beginning.

110

NOTES

Introduction

1. Edward W. Said, *Beginnings: Intention and Method* (New York: Basic Books, 1975), xiii.
2. Jacques Derrida, *Of Grammatology*, trans. Gayatri Chakravorty Spivak (Baltimore: Johns Hopkins Univ. Press, 1976).
3. The literature on Milton's debt to the Bible is extensive. See especially J[ohn] M[artin] Evans, *"Paradise Lost" and the Genesis Tradition* (Oxford: Clarendon Press, 1968), John T. Shawcross, *"Paradise Lost* and the Theme of the Exodus," *Milton Studies*, 2 (1970), 3–26, James H. Sims, *The Bible in Milton's Epics* (Gainesville: Univ. of Florida Press, 1962); on Milton's debt to the psalms, Mary Ann Radzinowicz, *Toward "Samson Agonistes": The Growth of Milton's Mind* (Princeton: Princeton Univ. Press, 1978); on the prophetic Milton, *Milton and the Line of Vision*, ed. Joseph A. Wittreich, Jr. (Madison: Univ. of Wisconsin Press, 1975), and William Kerrigan, *The Prophetic Milton* (Charlottesville: Univ. Press of Virginia, 1974); on Biblical genre, Barbara K. Lewalski, *Protestant Poetics and the Seventeenth-Century Religious Lyric* (Princeton: Princeton Univ. Press, 1979), and Lewalski, *"Paradise Lost" and the Rhetoric of Literary Forms* (Princeton: Princeton Univ. Press, 1985); on the priestly Milton, Michael Lieb, *Poetics of the Holy: A Reading of "Paradise Lost"* (Chapel Hill: Univ. of North Carolina Press, 1981). See also Wittreich, Jr., *Interpreting "Samson Agonistes"* (Princeton: Princeton Univ. Press, 1986), Mary Nyquist, "The Father's Word/Satan's Wrath," *PMLA*, 100, 2 (1985), 187–202, and a collection of intertextual studies, James H. Sims and Leland Ryken, *Milton and Scriptural Tradition: The Bible into Poetry* (Columbia: Univ. of Missouri Press, 1984).
4. "In a profound sense," writes Claus Westermann, "the Bible does not begin with Genesis, but with Exodus, not with the first article of faith ('I believe in God ... the Creator') but with the second ('historical redemption through her servant')." In Bernhard W. Anderson, *Creation versus Chaos: The Reinterpretation of Mythical Symbolism in the Bible* (New York: Association Press, 1967), 35–36. And according to Gerhard von Rad, the God who made the heavens and the earth is less often and less directly the object of faith than the God who brought his people out of Egypt. *Old Testament Theology*, trans. D. M. G. Stalker (New York: Harper and Brothers, 1962–65), vol. 1, 136–60.

5. *The Problem of the Hexateuch and Other Essays*, trans. E. W. Trueman Dicken (New York: McGraw-Hill, 1966), 1-78. While von Rad's traditio-historical method and his analysis of the Pentateuch have been challenged, his contribution on the place of the creation narratives in ancient Israel's sacred history is still valuable.
6. I refer to the so-called "Priestly" account of creation, Genesis 1:1-2:4a. The Yahwist's creation narrative, 2:4b-24, maintains the order of (1) creation (2) fall, even though man's position in the overall scheme of creation is inverted.
7. Geoffrey H. Hartman, "Milton's Counterplot," *ELH*, 25 (1958), 1-12.
8. Unless otherwise noted, all references to the Bible will be to the Revised Standard Version. While there is controversy over Milton's facility with rabbinic Hebrew (see Golda Speira Werman, "Midrash in *Paradise Lost: Capitula Rabbi Elieser*," *Milton Studies*, 18 [1983], 145-71), it is widely acknowledged that he read the Bible in the original. I am not privileging the translation of the Authorized Version because Milton relied heavily on the Hebrew text.
9. Unless otherwise noted, all references to Milton's prose are to *The Complete Prose Works of John Milton*, ed. Don M. Wolfe *et al.*, 8 vols. (New Haven: Yale Univ. Press, 1953-82), and will be cited in the text as *CP*, followed by volume and page. All references to poetry are to *John Milton: Complete Poems and Major Prose*, ed. Merritt Y. Hughes (New York: Odyssey Press, 1957), and will be cited hereafter as Hughes, followed by page.
10. On the Deuteronomic Moses, see James Nohrnberg, "Moses," in *Images of Man and God*, ed. Burke O. Long (Sheffield: Almond Press, 1981), 35-57, and Robert Polzin, *Moses and the Deuteronomist* (New York: Seabury Press, 1980). See also "On Literature and the Bible," *Centrum*, 2, 2 (1974), 5-43.
11. Stanley Fish, *Surprised by Sin: The Reader in "Paradise Lost"* (New York: St. Martin's Press, 1967).
12. The phrase is from Leslie Brisman's *Milton's Poetry of Choice and Its Romantic Heirs* (Ithaca: Cornell Univ. Press, 1973).

1 Milton's chaos: Chaos vs. creation

1. See J. H. Adamson, "Milton and the Creation," *Journal of English and Germanic Philology*, 61 (1962), 756-78.
2. Casaubon, *The Originall Cause of Temporall Evils* (London, 1645), the fifth page of the preface (n.p.) cited in Dennis Danielson, *Milton's Good God: A Study in Literary Theodicy* (Cambridge: Cambridge Univ. Press, 1982), 32-33.
3. A. S. P. Woodhouse, "Notes on Milton's Views on the Creation: The Initial Phase," *Philological Quarterly*, 28 (1949), 233.
4. Studies of the tradition include, along with Woodhouse's: A. B. Chambers, Jr., "Chaos in *Paradise Lost*," *Journal of the History of Ideas*, 24 (1963), 55-84; Walter Clyde Curry, "The Genesis of Milton's World," *Anglia*, 70 (1951), 129-49; Curry, *Milton's Ontology, Cosmogony, and Physics* (Lexington: Univ. of Kentucky Press, 1957); Michael Lieb, "Further Thoughts on Satan's Journey Through Chaos," *Milton*

Quarterly, 12 (1978), 126–33; Lieb, *The Dialectics of Creation: Patterns of Birth and Regeneration in "Paradise Lost"* (Amherst: Univ. of Massachusetts Press, 1970); and Danielson, 32–57. In a provocative paper, Robert M. Adams does focus on the chaos of Milton's epic; his interest is "not in where Milton got his Chaos but in what he did when he got it." "A Little Look into Chaos," in *Illustrious Evidence: Approaches to English Literature of the Early Seventeenth Century*, ed. Earl Miner (Berkeley: Univ. of California Press, 1975). He opens his paper lamenting the lack of critical interest in that subject: "It would have been nice to find other people's definitions, descriptions, and doctrines of Milton's Chaos, for guidance and support, as well as the always welcome occasions of polemic. But I was unable to find more than passing remarks on the subject, and will welcome suggestions as to where else I should look" (71). With gratitude for his contribution, I second the sentiment.

5. Adams, 76.
6. Lieb, *The Dialectics of Creation*, 16–17.
7. Chambers, 84.
8. Woodhouse, 229, n. 30.
9. Ibn Ezra, whose commentary, according to Fletcher, was written in the margin of Milton's Buxtorf rabbinic Bible. Harris Francis Fletcher, *Milton's Rabbinical Readings* (Urbana: Univ. of Illinois Press, 1930), 83.
10. Fletcher, 99.
11. Ernst Cassirer, *The Philosophy of Symbolic Forms*, trans. Ralph Manheim, vol. 2 of 3 vols., *Mythical Thought* (New Haven: Yale Univ. Press, 1955), 99.
12. Michael Lieb, *Poetics of the Holy: A Reading of "Paradise Lost"* (Chapel Hill: Univ. of North Carolina Press, 1981), 15. See also Lieb's helpful discussion of holiness in ancient Israel, 6–22.
13. Lev. 11:45 in Ronald Knox's version of the Old Testament, cited in Mary Douglas, *Purity and Danger: An Analysis of Concepts of Pollution and Taboo* (London: Routledge and Kegan Paul, 1966), 8.
14. Cassirer, 101.
15. Plotinus, *The Enneads*, trans. Stephen MacKenna, 3rd edn., rev. by B. S. Page (London: Faber and Faber, 1962), 68.
16. In her seminal analysis of the concept of pollution, *Purity and Danger*, Mary Douglas demonstrates that the Biblical notion of holiness suggests not just separation, but wholeness, completeness, "keeping distinct the categories of creation." See also Jean Soler, "The Dietary Prohibitions of the Hebrews," trans. E. Forster, *The New York Review of Books*, June 14, 1979, 24–30; and Julia Kristeva, *The Powers of Horror: An Essay on Abjection* (New York: Columbia Univ. Press, 1982).
17. Douglas, 41.
18. Michael Lieb comments that Adam and Eve become unclean upon violating God's command, noting that seventeenth-century commentators also made the connection between the forbidden fruit and the unclean food of Leviticus. In *The Forbidden Fruit: Or a Treatise of the Tree of Knowledge* (1640), Sebastian Frank writes that the fall was an "offense" to God, causing man to become "unclean": we shall become clean again

only when we "doe vomitt up the Fruit of the Tree of Knowledge of Good and Evill" (14–16). Lieb's interest is in the prohibition as "extra-legal and dispensational" – not in any of its commemorative impulses (Lieb, *Poetics of the Holy*, 114–18).

19. Michael Fixler, "The Unclean Meats of the Mosaic Law and the Banquet Scene in *Paradise Regained*," *Modern Language Notes*, 70 (1955), 573–77, 575.

20. In *Samson Agonistes*, the chorus ominously introduces Dalila: "But who is this, what thing of Sea or Land?" (710).

21. Kristeva, 90.

22. Arnold van Gennep, *The Rites of Passage*, trans. Monica B. Vizedom and Gabrielle L. Caffee (Chicago: Univ. of Chicago Press, 1960).

23. Victor Turner, *The Forest of Symbols: Aspects of Ndembu Ritual* (Ithaca: Cornell Univ. Press, 1967), 97. The following discussion draws upon Turner's chapter on liminality, "Betwixt and Between: The Liminal Period in Rites of Passage," 93–111.

24. Henry More, *An Appendix to the Defense of the Threefold Cabbala* (London, 1713), 185–86.

25. Adams, 76.

26. Turner, 97.

27. W. B. C. Watkins, *An Anatomy of Milton's Verse* (Baton Rouge: Louisiana State Univ. Press, 1955), 44, 42.

28. William Empson, *Milton's God* (London: Chatto & Windus, 1965, rev. edn.), 67.

29. Chambers, 66, and note.

30. Ps. 88:6, 69:15, John 2:3.

31. Isabel MacCaffrey points out Milton's debt to this Biblical formulation in *Paradise Lost as "Myth"* (Cambridge, Mass.: Harvard Univ. Press, 1959), 65, 66.

32. See Chambers, 61–65, where each position is summarized and evaluated. Chambers himself argues convincingly against Milton's primary debt to atomism and instead finds it in Plato's "receptacle."

33. *Ibid.*, 62.

34. Ralph Cudworth, *The True Intellectual System of the Universe* (London, 1678; facsimile rpt. New York and London: Garland Publishing, 1978). Vol. 1, chapter 2 is devoted to refuting the atomistic "atheistical doctrine."

35. Walter Charleton, *The Darkness of Atheism Dispelled by the Light of Nature* (London, 1652), 40–41. Discussed in Danielson, 33–34.

36. Titus Lucretius Carus, *On the Nature of Things*, trans. Thomas Jackson (Oxford, 1929), vol. 5, 421–31.

37. See S. K. Heninger, Jr., *The Cosmographical Glass: Renaissance Diagrams of the Universe* (San Marino: Huntington Library, 1977), 192–93. Heninger's comments here are accompanied by a fascinating diagram of atomistic cosmology: figure 117, "a world-system of the ancients" engraved by Wenceslaus Hollar for Sherburne's translation of *The Sphere* (London, 1675). The diagram depicts three concentric circles: the innermost includes the earth and planets, it is encircled by the "starry heaven" and, finally, both are encompassed by chaos, "in which this

World of ours is supposed to float, and of which it was composed, and into which in time it is to be resolved,'' according to the explanation accompanying the diagram.

38. Arnold Stein, "Satan's Metamorphoses: The Internal Speech,'' in *Milton Studies*, 1, ed. James D. Simmonds (Pittsburgh: Univ. of Pittsburgh Press, 1969), 94.

39. On the war in heaven, see Stella Revard, *The War in Heaven: "Paradise Lost" and the Tradition of Satan's Rebellion* (Ithaca: Cornell Univ. Press, 1980); James A. Freeman, *Milton and the Martial Muse: "Paradise Lost" and European Traditions of War* (Princeton: Princeton Univ. Press, 1980).

40. Dennis Burden, *The Logical Epic: A Study of the Argument of "Paradise Lost"* (Cambridge, Mass.: Harvard Univ. Press, 1967), 65. See 65–71 for his discussion of the distinction between providence and fate made throughout Milton's work. In *Lycidas*, "what the pastoral gods lack is a concept of providence: they can neither explain nor protect.''

41. See MacCaffrey, ch. 3, "Structural Patterns in *Paradise Lost*,'' 44–91.

42. The myth is translated in James B. Pritchard, ed., *Ancient Near Eastern Texts Relating to the Old Testament* (Princeton: Princeton Univ. Press, 1950; 2nd edn., 1955), 60–72. Thorkild Jacobsen understands the myth as reflecting the celebration of world order in *The Intellectual Adventure of Ancient Man*, ed. H. and H. A. Frankfort (Chicago: Univ. of Chicago Press, 1946). See also Alexander Heidel, *The Babylonian Genesis: The Story of Creation* (Chicago: Univ. of Chicago Press, 1951), and Ricoeur's discussion of the myth in *The Symbolism of Evil*, trans. Emerson Buchanan (Boston: Beacon Press, 1967).

43. The myth is translated by John Gray, *The Legacy of Canaan*, 2nd edn. (Leiden: E. J. Brill, 1965), 28. There is some debate over whether the Ugaritic myth focuses on the maintenance of order rather than its creation. Frank Cross, Jr., asserts that this myth is also cosmogonic, broadening our notion of what constitutes a "creation myth.'' *Canaanite Myth and Hebrew Epic* (Cambridge, Mass.: Harvard Univ. Press, 1973), 120.

44. See Heidel, 82–140, where he minimizes the connection between the Biblical creation account and ancient Near Eastern myth. E. O. James argues that the connection is much deeper in *Myth and Ritual in the Ancient Near East* (New York: Frederick A. Praeger, 1958), 198–99. E. A. Speiser, *Genesis*, vol. 1 in *The Anchor Bible Series* (Garden City, NY: Doubleday and Co., 1964) explores the Bible's debt to ancient Near Eastern parallels in detail.

45. In other Ugaritic texts, Lotan (the dragon), the ancestor of Leviathan, and Yamm (the sea) are conflated. The beast of Revelation 12, the dragon of Canaanite myth, and the chaos monster of Babylonian myth are all seven-headed. Isaiah has identified the Sea-monster with the dragon (Is. 27:1, 51:9–10) and Revelation has identified the dragon with Satan. See Cross, 119–20.

46. The Creation itself begins this process of historicization. As Frank Cross has suggested, "in the Israelite environment ... the beginning is 'merely' a first event in a historical sequence'' (120).

47. Ricoeur, 172.
48. I do not mean to deny the classical influence on Milton's chaos, but to correct the imbalance resulting from its sole emphasis.
49. Stanley Fish, *Surprised by Sin: The Reader in "Paradise Lost"* (New York: St. Martin's Press, 1967), 170.
50. Danielson, 28.
51. Ricoeur, 172.
52. The pioneering study of this theme is Hermann Gunkel's *Schöpfung und Chaos in Urzeit und Endzeit* (Göttingen: Vandenhoeck und Ruprecht, 1895).
53. Adams, 81 – 85.
54. Ricoeur, 178 – 79.
55. Cited in Barbara K. Lewalski, *Protestant Poetics and the Seventeenth-Century Religious Lyric* (Princeton: Princeton Univ. Press, 1979), 90.
56. Bernhard Anderson, *Creation versus Chaos: The Reinterpretation of Mythical Symbolism in the Bible* (New York: Association Press, 1967), 167.
57. Nicholas Berdjaev, *The Destiny of Man*, trans. Natalie Duddington (1955; rpt. New York: Harper & Row, 1960). "One may disagree with ... the Gnostics and Manichees, but one cannot help respecting them for their being so painfully conscious of the problem of evil" (23).
58. Woodhouse, 229, 230, n. 30 (last two ellipses in original).
59. On this controversy, see Victor Harris, *All Coherence Gone* (Chicago: Univ. of Chicago Press, 1949); Richard Foster Jones, *The Seventeenth Century* (Stanford: Stanford Univ. Press, 1951), 10 – 40; and *Ancients and Moderns* (St. Louis: Washington Univ. Studies, 1936), 22 – 40.
60. "The Almighty Father has taken thought for the universe, and set the stars more firmly in their place. He has poised the scales of destiny with a sure weight and commanded each thing to keep its course for ever in a supremely ordered whole." Trans. John Carey, *The Poems of John Milton*, ed. John Carey and Alastair Fowler (London: Longmans, Green and Co., 1968), 65.

2 "Secret gaze or open admiration": The invitation to origins

1. Arthur O. Lovejoy sees the implication of the dialogue as depicting God as a "humorous celestial sadist devising intellectual pitfalls for the human mind to provide amusement for himself" (140); therefore, he thinks that the dialogue has no place in the poem. "Milton's Dialogue on Astronomy," in *Reason and the Imagination*, ed. J. A. Mazzeo (New York: Columbia Univ. Press, 1962). Irene Samuel rescues Milton's anti-intellectual sounding remarks by defining the "lowly" of "be lowly wise" in a sense broad enough to include everything. "Milton on Learning and Wisdom," *PMLA*, 64 (1949), 708 – 23.
2. The theory that in the ensuing dialogue Milton takes on the "central astronomical dispute of his day" between the Ptolemaic and Copernican models has been discounted. Research into the prevailing models for the universe available to Milton has been conducted by Grant McColley,

"The Astronomy of *Paradise Lost*," *Studies in Philology*, 34 (1937), 209–47, who concludes that at least five different cosmological systems were available in Milton's age: the Copernican, the geo-heliocentric, the diurnal rotation of the earth, the Ptolemaic, and the doctrine of the plurality of worlds. Furthermore, the dialogue seems only to express cosmological commonplaces for it is drawn, often verbatim, from numerous sources, including Bishop John Wilkins, *The Discovery of a World in the Moone* (London, 1638), and Alexander Ross, *The New Planet No Planet: or, The Earth No Wandring Star* (London, 1646). See Grant McColley, "Milton's Dialogue on Astronomy: The Principle Immediate Sources," *PMLA*, 52 (1937), 728–62. Adam's question echoes that of John Wilkins: "Can we imagine that [nature] should appoint those numerous and vast bodies, the stars, to compass us with such a swift and restless motion, when as all this might as well be done by the revolution of this little ball of earth." Other works on Milton's astronomy include Allan H. Gilbert, "Milton's Textbook of Astronomy," *PMLA*, 38 (1923), 297–307, and "Milton and Galileo," *Studies in Philology*, 19 (1922), 152–85; Francis R. Johnson, *Astronomical Thought in Renaissance England* (Baltimore: Johns Hopkins Univ. Press, 1937); Marjorie Hope Nicholson, "The 'New Astronomy' and English Literary Imagination," *Studies in Philology*, 32 (1935), 428–62; "Milton and the Telescope," *ELH*, 2 (1935), 1–32, and *The Breaking of the Circle* (Evanston: Northwestern Univ. Press, 1950); Kester Svendson, *Milton and Science* (Cambridge, Mass.: Harvard Univ. Press, 1956); and Malabika Sarkar, " 'The Visible Diurnal Sphere': Astronomical Images of Space and Time in *Paradise Lost*," *Milton Quarterly*, 18 (1984), 1–5.

3. Svendson writes that either Milton's "ignorance of up-to-date astronomy or his disinclination to shift emphasis away from man dissuaded him from committing his poem to controversy" (45). Paul H. Kocher, *Science and Religion in Elizabethan England* (San Marino: Huntington Library, 1953), shows that for all its study of second causes, the age before Milton still clung to the divine impulse in nature. See "Science and Pseudo Science," in Arnold Williams, *The Common Expositor: An Account of the Commentaries on Genesis 1527–1633* (Chapel Hill: Univ. of North Carolina Press, 1948), 174–98.

4. Lovejoy, 142.

5. For the *Seventh Prolusion*, I have chosen the translation of Hughes, 625.

6. Svendsen, 44.

7. Hughes, 623.

8. I do not want to make Milton seem more coherent than he is. With his own system built upon origins and his active endeavor to inquire into them himself, this resistance to inquire into creation is especially intriguing. One could certainly argue that he is protecting himself from questions he can not answer. That "protection," however, is an extensive system rather than a thin justification.

9. See Don Cameron Allen, *The Legend of Noah: Renaissance Rationalism in Art, Science and Letters* (Urbana: University of Illinois Press, 1963), ch. 1;

Eugene F. Rice, Jr., *The Renaissance Idea of Wisdom* (Cambridge, Mass.: Harvard Univ. Press, 1958); Howard Schultz, *Milton and Forbidden Knowledge* (New York: Modern Language Association, 1955), ch. 1; Christian K. Zacker, *Curiosity and Pilgrimage* (Baltimore: Johns Hopkins Univ. Press, 1976), ch. 2; and Marcia L. Colish, *The Mirror of Language: A Study in the Medieval Theory of Knowledge* (New Haven: Yale Univ. Press, 1968).

10. Seneca, *Epistulae Morales*, xlviii, xlix, as cited in Schultz, 4, 5.
11. This opens Augustine's definition of wisdom in the *Contra Academicos*.
12. George Wither, *A Collection of Emblemes* (London, 1635), 147.
13. Eugene Rice writes that the antique belief in knowledge as an innate faculty was developed into a conception of knowledge as a revealed gift of grace by the Fathers but that it was "restored to its old autonomy and its purely human dignities" by the end of the Renaissance. Hans Blumenberg has refined this view in a recent major study, *The Legitimacy of the Modern Age*, trans. Robert M. Wallace (Cambridge, Mass.: MIT Press, 1983). See esp. Part III, "Curiosity Is Enrolled in the Catalogue of Vices" and "Difficulties Regarding the 'Natural' Status of the Appetite for Knowledge in the Scholastic Systems." He writes a history of philosophy from the Middle Ages to the Renaissance that charts the development in the belief in scientific curiosity, a process that describes the "legitimization" of the scientific age.
14. See Peter A. Fiore, *Milton and Augustine* (University Park: Pennsylvania State Univ. Press, 1981).
15. Schultz, 7–8.
16. Blumenberg, 311.
17. St. Augustine, *Confessions*, trans. R. S. Pine-Coffin (Baltimore: Penguin Books, 1961), 93. Augustine takes up the theme of curiosity in Books V and X.
18. *Ibid.*, 94.
19. *Ibid.*
20. Quoted from Hughes, 826.
21. Blumenberg delineates the steps: "in its extreme logical consequence (as Augustine defines it), curiosity subjects even God to the criterion of *utilitas*, so as to be able to seek *fruitio* in the human self alone" (312).
22. *Confessions*, 154.
23. *Christian Doctrine*, I. iv.
24. *Confessions*, 243.
25. "This futile curiosity masquerades under the name of science and learning, and since it derives from our thirst for knowledge and sight is the principal sense by which knowledge is acquired, in the Scriptures it is called *gratification of the eye.*" *Ibid.*, 241. He says that such curiosity takes an extreme form in the demand for the hidden God to show himself in miracles, "not in the hope of salvation, but simply for the love of the experience," (242). It is this curiosity that constitutes the final temptation of *Paradise Regained.*
26. Blumenberg, 310.
27. *Confessions*, 94.

28. This is one of the categories of epic that James Nohrnberg isolates in *The Analogy of the Faerie Queene* (Princeton: Princeton Univ. Press, 1976).
29. Freud, "Instincts and Their Vicissitudes," in *The Standard Edition of the Complete Psychological Works of Sigmund Freud*, trans. James Strachey (London: Hogarth Press, 1955), vol. 14, 127 (hereafter referred to as *SE*).
30. See Jacques Lacan, *The Four Fundamental Concepts of Psycho-Analysis*, ed. Jacques-Alain Miller, trans. Alan Sheridan (New York: W. W. Norton, 1978), 78. Lacan would regard fixation in voyeurism as a denial of the movements of substitution and repression characterizing shifts in positioning. The Lacanian "Gaze" suggests a whole system of shifts in voyeurism and exhibitionism – not strictly visual – in a largely unconscious discourse. See Robert Con Davis, "Lacan, Poe, and Narrative Repression," *Modern Language Notes*, 98, 5 (1983), 983–1005).
31. Edmund Bergler, *The Basic Neurosis: Oral Aggression and Psychic Masochism* (New York: Grune & Stratton, 1949), 189. David Walter Allen, *The Fear of Looking or Scopophilic – Exhibitionist Conflicts* (Charlottesville: Univ. of Virginia Press, 1974).
32. William Kerrigan has explored the key relation between guilty seeing and the primal scene in *The Sacred Complex: On the Psychogenesis of "Paradise Lost"* (Cambridge, Mass.: Harvard Univ. Press, 1983), in ch. 4, "The Way to Strength from Weakness," 127–92.
33. Chester McMullen has pursued this dynamic in an unpublished essay, "Blindness and the Book of God," Univ. of Colorado. He comes to the suggestive conclusion that the Son, as the seen God, is given up or sacrificed in the object position in order for the Father to remain concealed. "To be seen, is, to the voyeur, the ontological equivalent of death, and this seems to be precisely what God the Father is asking of God the Son when he asks for volunteers to redeem man" (21).
34. *At a Vacation Exercise*, ll. 34–35, 23–24.

3 "Remember and tell over": Creation in sacred song

1. Walter Schindler, *Voice and Crisis: Invocation in Milton's Poetry* (Hamden, Connecticut: Archon Books, 1984), 49–56. Schindler draws the kind of clean distinction between these adventures that I think Milton problematizes.
2. Jonathan Culler, "Apostrophe," in *The Pursuit of Signs* (Ithaca: Cornell Univ. Press, 1981), 142.
3. *Ibid.*, 140.
4. *Ibid.*, 146.
5. Sigmund Mowinckel, *The Psalms in Israel's Worship*, trans. D. R. Ap-Thomas, 2 vols. (Oxford: Basil Blackwell, 1962), vol. 1, 81–90.
6. Bronislaw Malinowski, *Coral Gardens and Their Magic*, 2 vols. (1935; rpt. New York: Dover, 1978), vol. 2, 55.
7. Whether or not Milton's invocations "work" can be understood in two senses: first, do they conform to the conventions of invocation so that readers who share a consensus about the form can recognize them as such, and second, do they work in the sense of provoking an answer.

Fish would include the former in the province of speech-act theory but not the latter. "What [speech-act theory] can do is ... provide analyses of conventional performances" but, "just as it stops short of claiming knowledge of what happens after the performance of an illocutionary act, so is it silent on the question of what ... preceded it" (227). But it is precisely his distinction between "uptake" (understanding an utterance as conforming to a convention) and "reaction" (the response an utterance provokes) that is so often blurred in the Bible. The debate about whether Milton's poem works as an epic seems to have calmed, but whether or not it "works" in that other sense – does it redeem its author and its hearers – is surely beyond the province of speech-act theory. "How To Do Things with Austin and Searle: Speech-Act Theory and Literary Criticism," in *Is There a Text in This Class? The Authority of Interpretive Com-munities* (Cambridge, Mass.: Harvard Univ. Press, 1980), 197–245.

8. See J. L. Austin, *How To Do Things with Words* (Cambridge, Mass.: Harvard Univ. Press, 1962); a response by Jacques Derrida, "Signature, Event, Context," *Glyph*, 1 (1977), 172–97; a response to Derrida's essay by John Searle, "Reiterating the Differences: A Reply to Derrida," *Glyph*, 1 (1977), 198–208; Derrida, "Limited Inc.," *Glyph*, 2 (1977), 162–254; and a discussion of the debate in Stanley Fish, "With the Compliments of the Author: Reflections on Austin and Derrida," *Critical Inquiry*, 8 (1982), 693–721.

9. Georgia Christopher, in *Milton and the Science of the Saints* (Princeton: Princeton Univ. Press, 1982), writes about the dynamic character of words, grounding her discussion in Reformation doctrine. See esp. chs. 1 and 4.

10. *Martin Luther's Werke* 3, 154, 7. Weimar Edition of Luther's Works (Weimar: Bohlau, 1938).

11. *The New Creatue* (London, 1633), 166, cited in John R. Knott, Jr., *The Sword of the Spirit: Puritan Responses to the Bible* (Chicago: Univ. of Chicago Press, 1980), 8. Knott has demonstrated the pervasiveness among Puritans of one metaphor for the effective word, the word as weapon.

12. See Fish's discussion of the debtate, "With the Compliments of the Author: Reflections on Austin and Derrida," 701.

13. Derrida, "Signature, Event, Context," 190. While Austin writes that "infelicity is an ill to which all acts are heir which have the general character of ritual or ceremony" (18, 19), Derrida understands "ritual" as not the circumstances surrounding an utterance, but the "structural characteristic of every mark" (189).

14. Of course, Derrida would not say that interpretative problems need to be "infused," because the issue of interpretation is always there in every utterance; Satan only exploits a condition of all language.

15. Michel de Certeau, "What We Do When We Believe," in Marshall Blonsky, ed., *On Signs* (Baltimore: Johns Hopkins Univ. Press, 1985), 195–96.

16. Emile Benveniste, *Le Vocabulaire des institutions indo-européennes* (Paris: Minuit, 1969), vol. 1, ch. 15, 171–79, cited in de Certeau, 192.

17. De Certeau, 192–93.

18. Quoted from Hughes, 817.

19. *The English Poems of George Herbert*, ed. C. A. Patrides (London: J. M. Dent, 1974), 129.
20. In his analysis of the poem, R. W. Condee, *Structure in Milton's Poetry: From the Foundation to the Pinnacles* (University Park: Pennsylvania State Univ. Press, 1974), discusses the weakness in structure resulting from Milton's anticlimactic order.
21. For a full discussion of the Priestly Milton, the poet as *sacerdos*, see "Sacred Poetics" in Michael Lieb, *Poetics of the Holy: A Reading of "Paradise Lost"* (Chapel Hill: Univ. of North Carolina, 1981), 43–85.
22. Milton's prophetic role has also been extensively treated. See William Kerrigan, *The Prophetic Milton* (Charlottesville: Univ. Press of Virginia, 1974); Joseph A. Wittreich, Jr., *Milton and the Line of Vision* (Madison: Univ. of Wisconsin Press, 1975); and Wittreich, Jr., *Visionary Poetics: Milton's Tradition and His Legacy* (San Marino: Huntington Library, 1979).
23. Paul Humbert compares Genesis 1 and Psalm 104, concluding that both are liturgical texts drawn from the Israelite New Year festival. The seven-day scheme of Genesis reflects the seven days of the Feast of Tabernacles with which the New Year begins. "La Relation de Genèse 1 et du Psaume 104 avec la liturgie du Nouvel-An israelite," in *Opouscles d'un Hebriasant* (Université de Neuchâtel, 1958), 60–82, cited in Bernhard W. Anderson, *Creation versus Chaos: The Reinterpretation of Mythical Symbolism in the Bible* (New York: Association Press, 1967), 83. Both Gunkel and Ricoeur have noted that Genesis 1 echoes the *Enuma Elish* which was read during the Akitu, the Babylonian New Year festival. The implicit issue here is the rich relation between story and ritual, whether story is seen as "script" for enactment, or if narrative "performs" a ritual itself.
24. Paul Ricoeur, *The Symbolism of Evil*, trans. Emerson Buchanan (Boston: Beacon Press, 1967), 192.
25. The relation between performatives and ritual is not accidental. Because specific conventions must link words to institutional procedures, "performatives are, if one likes, just rather special sorts of ceremony." Stephen Levinson, *Pragmatics* (Cambridge: Cambridge Univ. Press, 1983), 230–31.
26. Mircea Eliade's discussion of "The Regeneration of Time" in his classic *The Myth of the Eternal Return* is still helpful. Trans. Willard R. Trask (New York: Pantheon, 1954), 51–91, esp. 76.
27. The imperfect tense of the Hebrew verbs in Psalm 104, a psalm to creation, reflect this sense of continual creative activity. Anderson, 93.
28. Edward Said, *Beginnings: Intention and Method* (New York: Basic Books, 1975); Jacques Derrida, *Of Grammatology*, trans. Gayatri Chakravorty Spivak (Baltimore: Johns Hopkins Univ. Press, 1982). Ritual offers an understanding of iteration that is deeply allied to postmodern thought.
29. *Divine Weeks and Works*, trans. Joshua Sylvester (1605: facsimile rpt., Gainesville: Scholars' Facsimiles and Reprints, 1965), 245, lettering modernized.
30. "As for the Divine Service and Common Prayer, it is so chaunted and minsed and mangled of our costly hired, curious, and nice Musitiens

(not to instruct the audience withall, nor to stirre up mens mindes unto devotion, but with a whorish harmony to tickle their eares:) that it must justly seeme not to be a noyse made of men, but rather a bleating of bruite beasts; whiles the Coristers ney descant as it were a sort of Colts; others bellowe a tenour, as it were a company of oxen: others barke a counterpoint, as it were a kennell of Dogs: others rore out a treble like a sort of Buls: others grunt out a base as it were a number of Hogs; so that a foule evill favoured noyse is made, but as for the wordes and sentences and the very matter it selfe, is nothing understanded at all; but the authority and power of judgment is taken away both from the minde and from the eares utterly." Cited by Percy A. Scholes, *The Puritans and Music in England and New England* (London: Oxford Univ. Press, 1934), 218.

31. Cited by Jocelyn Perkins, *Westminster Abbey: Its Worship and Ornaments*, 3 vols. (London: Oxford Univ. Press (1938 – 52), vol. 3, 111.
32. See Laurence Stapleton, "Milton and the New Music," *University of Toronto Quarterly*, 23 (1953 – 54), 217 – 26. Stapleton distinguishes the "enchantment of good" which can evoke a raptus of contemplation that leads to God from the enchantment of evil which "dulls and lessens our humanity."
33. Leo Spitzer, "Classical and Christian Ideas of World Harmony," *Traditio*, 2 (1944), 409 – 64; 3 (1945), 307 – 64 (New York: Cosmopolitan Science and Art Service Co., Inc.). John Hollander, *The Untuning of the Sky: Ideas of Music in English Poetry, 1500 – 1700* (Princeton: Princeton Univ. Press, 1961).
34. Spitzer, *Traditio*, 3, 315 – 316.
35. *Ibid.*, 335.
36. Cowley also describes creation as music in *Davideis*.
37. George Wither, *A Preparation to the Psalter* (London, 1619; facsimile rpt., Manchester: Charles E. Simms, 1884), 11, 12, lettering modernized.
38. Barbara K. Lewalski, *Milton's Brief Epic: The Genre, Meaning, and Art of "Paradise Regained"* (Providence: Brown Univ. Press, 1966).
39. Augustine, *Confessions*, 21.
40. The Biblical scholar Claus Westermann writes of Genesis, "Praise of God, the Creator, does not presuppose the creation story, but quite the reverse: praise of God is the source and presupposition of the creation story. The present narrative is, in fact, a developed and expanded confession of faith in God as Creator." *A Thousand Years and a Day: Our Time in the Old Testament*, trans. Stanley Rudman (Philadelphia: Muhlenberg Press, 1962), 3.
41. Nonetheless, all three movements share a common image pattern, contrasting the images of light and harmony with images of gloom and discord. Arthur Barker, "The Pattern of Milton's *Nativity Ode*," *University of Toronto Quarterly*, 10 (1940 – 41), 173.
42. A. S. P. Woodhouse, "Notes on Milton's Early Development," *University of Toronto Quarterly*, 13 (1943 – 4), 92.
43. Edward W. Tayler, *Milton's Poetry: Its Development in Time* (Pittsburgh: Dusquesne Univ. Press, 1979), 34 – 40.

Notes to pages 82–85

44. *Ibid.*, 35.
45. Mary Ann Radzinowicz, *Toward "Samson Agonistes": The Growth of Milton's Mind* (Princeton: Princeton Univ. Press, 1978), 195.
46. Fowler comments on this in his note to III, 410–15. *Paradise Lost*, ed. Alastair Fowler (London: Longman, 1968), 167.
47. *Confessions*, 26.
48. Samuel Johnson deemed the function of prayer and of *Paradise Lost* to be an acknowledgment of contingency. "Johnson may think that the different arts of praying and of making poems approach each other more nearly and more successfully in *Paradise Lost* than in any other poem he analyzed." Stephen Fix, "Johnson and the 'Duty' of Reading *Paradise Lost*," *ELH*, 52, 3 (1985), 658.
49. This liturgical character has been remarked upon by Michael Fixler. He begins an essay on the apocalyptic: "I had intended to argue that Milton conceived *Paradise Lost* as an act of worship, and that its sacramental character made it an early and significant instance of the deliberate substitution of literary for liturgical communion – in short of the religion of art" (131). Fixler still maintains this conviction, even while he elects to focus on the role of Revelation in *Paradise Lost* instead. "The Apocalypse within *Paradise Lost*," in *New Essays on "Paradise Lost"*, ed. Thomas Kranidas (Berkeley: Univ. of California Press, 1969), 131–78. See also Thomas B. Stroup, *Religious Rite and Ceremony in Milton's Poetry* (Lexington: Univ. of Kentucky Press, 1968). Stroup charts Milton's allusions to liturgy throughout, but he is over-cautious in his conclusion that "Milton's forms are basically secular."
50. *Protestant Poetics and the Seventeenth-Century Religious Lyric* (Princeton: Princeton Univ. Press, 1979), 316. Chana Bloch, in *Spelling the Word: George Herbert and the Bible* (Berkeley: Univ. of California Press, 1985), makes a similar observation about Herbert's *The Temple* in her final chapter, describing how he transformed the psalms into "Christian songs of praise." Yoking Herbert's poetry to the psalms has other critical precedent: Bloch cites Martz's interest in echoes (232).
51. The exception is Mary Ann Radzinowicz who has called attention to the "progress of the soul" characterizing an embedded narrative in the psalms in *Toward "Samson Agonistes."* Radzinowicz demonstrates that Milton's debt to the psalms is much greater than previously recognized. In addition to charting the extensive allusions to the psalms in *Samson Agonistes*, she asserts that he drew upon the psalms in poems not self-evidently indebted to them.
52. Raymond B. Waddington, "Milton Among the Carolines," in *The Age of Milton*, ed. C. A. Patrides and Raymond B. Waddington (Manchester: Manchester Univ. Press, 1980), 343–44.
53. In his study of the genre of praise, *The Enduring Monument: A Study of the Idea of Praise in Renaissance Literary Theory and Practice* (Chapel Hill: Univ. of North Carolina Press, 1962), O. B. Hardison schematizes Artistotle's history of literary kinds:

Praise	Blame
Hymns and panegyrics	Invective
Heroic poetry	Comic epic
Epic	Satire
Tragedy	Comedy

The division between the basic categories – the representation of noble and ignoble actions – is more significant than any within those spheres (28).

54. *Ibid.*, 69–70.
55. George Puttenham, *The Arte of English Poesie*, 1589, in *Elizabethan Critical Essays*, ed. George Gregory Smith (London: Oxford Univ. Press, 1904), vol. 2, 31.
56. "For what els is the awaking his musicall instruments; the often and free changing of persons; his notable *Prosopopeias*, when he maketh you, as it were, see God comming in his Maiestie; his telling of the Beastes ioyfulnes, and hills leaping, but a heauenlie poesie." Sir Philip Sidney, "An Apologie for Poetrie," 1595, in *ibid.*, vol. 1, 155.
57. Wither, *A Preparation to the Psalter*, 71.
58. This figure is from *The Short Title Catalogue*. See Coburn Freer, *Music for a King: George Herbert's Styles and the Metrical Psalms* (Baltimore: Johns Hopkins Univ. Press, 1972), 15.
59. Lewalski, *Protestant Poetics and the Seventeenth-Century Religious Lyric*. See esp. her chapter "Biblical Genre Theory," 31–71. Lewalski regards the psalms as one of the Biblical genres that inspired the seventeenth-century lyric.
60. Freer, 15.
61. Besides the legacy left by the anonymous biographer, biography and history offer another key to Milton's interest in the psalms. Milton's youthful paraphrases of Psalms 114 and 136 were placed at the beginning of the 1645 volume with the proud headnote: "This and the following Psalm were done by the Author at fifteen years old." He translated Psalms 80 through 88, dating them April 1648, and five years later he translated another group, Psalms 1 through 8. Just why he chose to translate these particular psalms at these particular times has invited speculation. The themes of these psalms – enslavement by enemies, unjust persecution of the servants of God, interference with the right worship of God made them especially apposite. In 1648, the Royalist threat was tangible, the Scots were amassing an army to invade England in defense of the King; Parliament had voted not to alter the government of the country and to put aside the No-Address Resolution which would have blocked communications with the King. Furthermore, the Ordinance for the Suppression of Blasphemie and Heresies was passed, reviving the threat of enforced conformity. "Milton's choice seems securely attached to the contemporary occasion," according to Radzinowicz; Collette maintains that in these psalms, "Milton was meditating on the dangers which threatened England and confronting those dangers through prayer" (253).

The bibliography on Milton's psalm translation includes: Carolyn Collette, "Milton's Psalm Translations: Petition and Praise," *English*

Literary Renaissance, 2 (1972), 243–59; William B. Hunter, Jr., "Milton Translates the Psalms," *Philological Quarterly*, 40 (1961), 485–94; Radzinowicz, "Biblical Poetry and Medicinal Truth," in *Toward "Samson Agonistes"*, 188–208; and M. H. Studley, "Milton and His Paraphrases of the Psalms," *Philological Quarterly*, 4 (1925), 364–72.

62. George Wither, *Psalmes of David* (rpt. New York: Burt Franklin, 1967), sig. A.6.

63. John Donne, *The Sermons of John Donne*, ed. G. R. Potter and Evelyn M. Simpson, 10 vols. (Berkeley: Univ. of California Press, 1953–62), vol. 5, 270–71.

64. Lewalski, *Protestant Poetics and the Seventeenth-Century Religious Lyric*, 50.

65. Martin Luther, *A Manual of the Book of Psalms*, trans. Henry Cole (London, 1837), 5.

66. Radzinowicz, 193.

67. In the mid-1640s, the translation of the psalter had become a project of national concern. Extant versions were deemed unsatisfactory (a pamphlet was circulated entitled "Reasons Against the Reception of King James' Metaphrase of the Psalms"), and in 1643 the Westminster Assembly of Divines convened to begin plans for the preparation of a new psalter. The version that resulted was also poorly received, and another revised version was recommended. It was in April 1648 that those appointed for the task first reported to the Assembly. The fact that Milton began his mature psalm translations with Psalm 80 supports the hypothesis that he hoped to contribute to the national psalter, for that psalm marked one of the major divisions in the translation to be done by committee.

68. There are only two references to David in *Paradise Lost* and they occur in the Biblical history Michael unfolds to Adam in the concluding books. In *Paradise Regained*, there are more allusions to David, but these are to David's throne.

69. Sir Philip Sidney, *An Apologie for Poetrie*, 1595, in *Elizabethan Critical Essays* ed. George Gregory Smith (London: Oxford Univ. Press, 1904), vol. 1, 151–2.

70. In Ficino's doctrine of *furores*, poets possess not only poetic but religious, prophetic furor. His example is Orpheus: "Omnibus his furoribus occupatum fuisse Orpheum libri eius testimonio esse possunt." *Opera Omnia* (Basle, 1576), II. 1362. Pico writes, "Sicut hymni David operi Cabalae mirabiliter deserviunt, ita hymni Orphei operi verè licitae & naturalis Magiae." *Opera Omnia* (Basle, 1572), I. 106. See D. P. Walker's thorough study of the reception and application of the Orpheus tradition in the Renaissance. "Orpheus the Theologian and Renaissance Platonists," *Journal of the Warburg and Courtauld Institutes*, 16 (1953), 100–20.

71. Marot, *Oeuvres*, ed. Guiffrey (Paris, 1875–1931), V. 198–9, cited in Walker, 101.

72. La Boderie, *L'Encyclie des Decrets de l'Eternité* (Antwerp, n.d. [privilege dated Oct. 1570]), 189, cited in Walker, 101.

73. See the illuminating discussion of Milton's use of the Orpheus myth

by Caroline W. Mayerson, "The Orpheus Image in *Lycidas*," *PMLA*, 64 (1949), 189–207.

74. Dennis Burden, *The Logical Epic: A Study of the Argument of "Paradise Lost"* (Cambridge, Mass.: Harvard Univ. Press, 1967).

4 "Yet once more": Re-creation, repetition, and return

1. Edward W. Said, *Beginnings: Intention and Method* (New York: Basic Books 1975), 280.
2. Paul Ricoeur, *The Symbolism of Evil*, trans. Emerson Buchanan (Boston: Beacon Press, 1967), 169–70. See also his monumental study of *Time and Narrative*, 2 vols., trans. Kathleen McLaughlin and David Pellauer (Chicago: Univ. of Chicago Press, 1984), where his presupposition is that "the world unfolded by every narrative work is always a temporal world." And that "time becomes human time to the extent that it is organized after the manner of a narrative; narrative, in turn, is meaningful to the extent that it portrays the features of temporal experience" (3).
3. Freud, *Beyond the Pleasure Principle*, trans. James Strachey (New York: W. W. Norton, 1961).
4. Paul Ricoeur, *Freud and Philosophy*, trans. Denis Savage (New Haven: Yale Univ. Press, 1970), 282–87.
5. *Ibid.*, 284.
6. Freud, *Beyond the Pleasure Principle*, 26.
7. Derrida has challenged the notion that Freud is moving beyond the pleasure principle, demonstrating that despite the appearance of "steps" in his argument, he is confirming the authority of the PP, playing the *fort-da* game himself with something beyond the pleasure principle. "Coming into One's Own," trans. James Hulbert, in Geoffrey H. Hartman (ed.), *Psychoanalysis and the Question of the Text* (Baltimore: Johns Hopkins Univ. Press, 1978), 114–48.
8. Jean Laplanche, *Life and Death in Psychoanalysis*, trans. Jeffrey Mehlman (Baltimore: Johns Hopkins Univ. Press, 1976).
9. *Freud and Philosophy*, 292.
10. Joseph H. Smith, "Rite, Ritual, and Defense," *Psychiatry*, 46 (1983), 18.
11. Nietzsche, *Thus Spoke Zarathustra*, in *The Portable Nietzsche*, trans. Walter Kaufman (New York: Viking Press, 1954), 251–52. Of course, Nietzsche's thought here is Satanic rather than Miltonic. For Nietzsche, we can overcome the pastness of the past – by willing the eternal return of the same.
12. *Ibid.*
13. Freud, *Beyond the Pleasure Principle*.
14. Play can be seen as not simply ineffectual, but as an important sphere in which acts can be repeated, experiments and innovations achieved, without the pressure of imperative needs. See Smith, 17.
15. Victor Turner, *The Forest of Symbols: Aspects of Ndembu Ritual* (Ithaca: Cornell Univ. Press, 1967), 97.
16. "Milton," from *The Lives of the English Poets*, in *Milton Criticism: Selections*

Notes to pages 99 – 109

from Four Centuries, ed. James Thorpe (New York: Rinehart & Co., Inc., 1950), 83.

17. Angus Fletcher, *Allegory: The Theory of a Symbolic Mode* (Ithaca: Cornell Univ. Press, 1964), 181–95.

18. Otto Rank, *The Double: A Psychoanalytic Study*, trans. Harry Tucker, Jr. (Chapel Hill: Univ. of North Carolina Press, 1971). Freud, "The Uncanny," in *SE*, vol. 17, 219–52. The compelled and unconscious nature of doubling and repetition surround both with an aura of the "uncanny" and a sense of the "daemonic." We are not so far from Freud's own terminology to speak of "Satanic repetition."

19. John T. Irwin, *Doubling and Incest/Repetition and Revenge: A Speculative Reading of Faulkner* (Baltimore: Johns Hopkins Univ. Press, 1975), 43.

20. Rank, 72–73.

21. See James W. Earl, "Eve's Narcissism," *Milton Quarterly*, 19 (1985), 13–16, where the scene is no "correction of moral error, but psychological growth."

22. Rank, 73–77, and Irwin, 33.

23. Rank, 77.

24. *Ibid.*, 78.

25. Smith, 18.

26. See Hannah Arendt, *The Life of the Mind, Vol. II: Willing* (New York: Harcourt Brace Jovanovich, 1978), 158.

27. Hans W. Loewald, "Some Considerations on Repetition and Repetition Compulsion," *International Journal of Psycho-Analysis*, 52 (1971), 59–66.

28. See Milton's *Christian Doctrine*, I. xix.

29. Freud, "'Remembering, Repeating, and Working-Through," in *SE*, vol. 12, 150.

30. Ricoeur, *Freud and Philosophy*, 286.

31. Loewald, 62.

32. *Ibid.*, 63.

33. The literature on the symbolism of light is extensive. See especially William Kerrigan, *The Sacred Complex: On the Psychogenesis of "Paradise Lost"* (Cambridge, Mass.: Harvard Univ. Press, 1983), pp. 142–92, where the invocation to light is part of a logic of renovation for the poet, a "way to strength from weakness." Michael Lieb's discussions of light, *Poetics of the Holy: A Reading of "Paradise Lost"* (Chapel Hill: Univ. of North Carolina Press, 1981), 185–210, 212–45, place Milton's understanding in the rich Biblical and philosophical traditions. Also helpful are: Don Cameron Allen, *Harmonious Vision: Studies in Milton's Poetry* (Baltimore: Johns Hopkins Univ. Press, 1970), 122–42; Merritt Y. Hughes, "Milton and the Symbol of Light," in *Ten Perspectives on Milton* (New Haven: Yale Univ. Press, 1965), 62; A. B. Chambers, Jr., "Wisdom at One Entrance Quite Shut Out," *Philological Quarterly*, 42 (1963), 114–19.

34. Smith, 20.

35. Ricoeur, *Freud and Philosophy*, 286.

36. *The City of God*, ed. Vernon J. Bourke (New York: Doubleday, 1958), 542.

37. *Ibid.*
38. *Ibid.*, 343.
39. Loewald, 59–66.
40. *The City of God*, ed. Bourke, 343.
41. *Ibid.*, 544–45.

WORKS CITED

Adams, Robert M. "A Little Look into Chaos." In *Illustrious Evidence: Approaches to English Literature of the Early Seventeenth Century*. Ed. Earl Miner. Berkeley: Univ. of California Press, 1975, 71–89.

Adamson, J. H. "Milton and the Creation." *JEGP*, 61 (1962), 756–78.

Allen, David Walton. *The Fear of Looking or Scopophilic–Exhibitionist Conflicts*. Charlottesville: Univ. of Virginia Press, 1974.

Allen, Don Cameron. *Harmonious Vision: Studies in Milton's Poetry*. Baltimore: Johns Hopkins Univ. Press, 1970.

The Legend of Noah: Renaissance Rationalism in Art, Science and Letters. Urbana: Univ. of Illinois Press, 1963.

Anderson, Bernhard. *Creation versus Chaos: The Reinterpretation of Mythical Symbolism in the Bible*. New York: Association Press, 1967.

Arendt, Hannah. *The Life of the Mind, Vol. II: Willing*. New York: Harcourt Brace Jovanovich, 1978.

Augustinus, Aurelius, Saint, bishop of Hippo (Saint Augustine). *The City of God*. Ed. Vernon J. Bourke. New York: Doubleday, 1958.

Confessions. Trans. R. S. Pine-Coffin. Baltimore: Penguin Books, 1961.

Austin, J. L. *How To Do Things with Words*. Cambridge, Mass.: Harvard Univ. Press, 1962.

Barker, Arthur. "The Pattern of Milton's *Nativity Ode*." *Univ. of Toronto Quarterly*, 10 (1940–41), 167–81.

Benveniste, Emile. *Le Vocabulaire des institutions indo-européennes*. Paris: Minuit, 1969.

Berdjaev, Nicholas. *The Destiny of Man*. Trans. Natalie Duddington. 1955; rpt. New York: Harper & Row, 1960.

Bergler, Edmund. *The Basic Neurosis: Oral Agression and Psychic Masochism*. New York: Grune & Stratton, 1949.

Bloch, Chana. *Spelling the Word: George Herbert and the Bible*. Berkeley: Univ. of California Press, 1985.

Blonsky, Marshall, ed. *On Signs*. Baltimore: Johns Hopkins Univ. Press, 1985.

Blumenberg, Hans. *The Legitimacy of the Modern Age*. Trans. Robert M. Wallace. Cambridge, Mass.: MIT Press, 1983.

Brisman, Leslie. *Milton's Poetry of Choice and Its Romantic Heirs*. Ithaca: Cornell Univ. Press, 1973.

Burden, Dennis. *The Logical Epic: A Study of the Argument of "Paradise Lost"*. Cambridge, Mass.: Harvard Univ. Press, 1967.

Carey, John, and Fowler, Alastair, eds. *The Poems of John Milton*. Trans. John Carey. London: Longmans, Green and Co., 1968.

Carus, Titus Lucretius. *On the Nature of Things*. Trans. Thomas Jackson. Vol. 5. Oxford, 1929.

Casaubon, Meric. *The Originall Cause of Temporall Evils*. London, 1645.

Cassirer, Ernst. *The Philosophy of Symbolic Forms*. Trans. Ralph Manheim. Vol. 2: *Mythical Thought*. New Haven: Yale Univ. Press, 1955.

Certeau, Michel de. "What We Do When We Believe." In Marshall Blonsky, ed. *On Signs*. Baltimore: Johns Hopkins Univ. Press, 1985.

Chambers, A. B., Jr. "Chaos in *Paradise Lost*." *Journal of the History of Ideas*, 24 (1963), 55–84.

"Wisdom at One Entrance Quite Shut Out." *Philological Quarterly*, 42 (1963), 114–19.

Charleton, Walter. *The Darkness of Atheism Dispelled by the Light of Nature*. London, 1652.

Christopher, Georgia. *Milton and the Science of the Saints*. Princeton: Princeton Univ. Press, 1982.

Colie, Rosalie. *The Resources of Kind: Genre-Theory in the Renaissance*. Berkeley: Univ. of California Press, 1973.

Colish, Marcia L. *The Mirror of Language: A Study in the Medieval Theory of Knowledge*. New Haven: Yale Univ. Press, 1968.

Collette, Carolyn. "Milton's Psalm Translations: Petition and Praise." *English Literary Renaissance*, 2 (1972), 243–59.

Condee, R. W. *Structure in Milton's Poetry: From the Foundation to the Pinnacles*. University Park: Pennsylvania State Univ. Press, 1974.

Cross, Frank, Jr. *Canaanite Myth and Hebrew Epic*. Cambridge, Mass.: Harvard Univ. Press, 1973.

Cudworth, Ralph. *The True Intellectual System of the Universe*. London, 1678: facsimile rpt. New York and London: Garland Publishing, 1978.

Culler, Jonathan. *The Pursuit of Signs*. Ithaca: Cornell Univ. Press, 1981.

Curry, Walter Clyde. "The Genesis of Milton's World." *Anglia*, 70 (1951), 129–49.

Milton's Ontology, Cosmogony, and Physics. Lexington: Univ. of Kentucky Press, 1957.

Danielson, Dennis. *Milton's Good God: A Study in Literary Theodicy*. Cambridge: Cambridge Univ. Press, 1982.

Davies, Robert Con. "Lacan, Poe, and Narrative Repression." *Modern Language Notes*, 98, 5 (1983), 983–1005.

Derrida, Jacques. *Of Grammatology*. Trans. Gayatri Chakravorty Spivak. Baltimore: Johns Hopkins Univ. Press, 1976.

"Limited Inc." *Glyph*, 2 (1977), 162–254.

"Signature, Event, Context." *Glyph*, 1 (1977), 172–97.

Donne, John. *The Sermons of John Donne*. Ed. G. R. Potter and Evelyn M. Simpson. 10 vols. Berkeley: Univ. of California Press, 1953–62.

Douglas, Mary. *Purity and Danger: An Analysis of Concepts of Pollution and Taboo*. London: Routledge and Kegan Paul, 1966.

Du Bartas. *Divine Weeks and Works*. Trans. Joshua Sylvester. 1605; facsimile rpt., Gainesville: Scholars, Facsimiles and Reprints, 1965.

Works cited

Earl, James W. "Eve's Narcissism." *Milton Quarterly*, 19 (1985), 13–16.

Eliade, Mircea. *The Myth of the Eternal Return*. Trans. Willard R. Trask. New York: Pantheon, 1954.

Empson, William. *Milton's God*. London: Chatto & Windus, 1965, rev. edn.

Evans, J[ohn] M[artin]. *"Paradise Lost" and the Genesis Tradition*. Oxford: Clarendon Press, 1968.

Fiore, Peter A. *Milton and Augustine*. University Park: Pennsylvania State Univ. Press, 1981.

Fish, Stanley, *Is There a Text in This Class? The Authority of Interpretive Communities*. Cambridge, Mass.: Harvard Univ. Press, 1980.

Surprised by Sin: The Reader in "Paradise Lost." New York: St. Martin's Press, 1967.

"With the Compliments of the Author: Reflections on Austin and Derrida." *Critical Inquiry*, 8 (1982), 693–721.

Fix, Stephen. "Johnson and the 'Duty' of Reading *Paradise Lost*." *ELH*, 52 (1985), 649–71.

Fixler, Michael. "The Apocalypse within *Paradise Lost*." In *New Essays on "Paradise Lost"*. Ed. Thomas Kranidas. Berkeley: Univ. of California Press, 1969, 131–78.

"The Unclean Meats of the Mosaic Law and the Banquet Scene in *Paradise Regained*." *Modern Language Notes*, 70 (1955), 573–77.

Fletcher, Angus. *Allegory: The Theory of a Symbolic Mode*. Ithaca: Cornell Univ. Press, 1964.

Fletcher, Harris Francis. *Milton's Rabbinical Readings*. Urbana: Univ. of Illinois Press, 1930.

Freeman, James A. *Milton and the Martial Muse: "Paradise Lost" and European Traditions of War*. Princeton: Princeton Univ. Press, 1980.

Freer, Coburn. *Music for a King: George Herbert's Styles and the Metrical Psalms*. Baltimore: Johns Hopkins Univ. Press, 1972.

Freud, Sigmund. *Beyond the Pleasure Principle*. Trans. James Strachey. New York: W.W. Norton, 1961.

"Remembering, Repeating, and Working-Through." In *The Standard Edition of the Complete Psychological Works of Sigmund Freud*. Trans. James Strachey. London: Hogarth Press, 1955. Vol. 12, 147–56.

"Instincts and Their Vicissitudes." In *The Standard Edition*. Vol. 14, 111–40.

"The Uncanny." In *The Standard Edition*. Vol. 17, 219–52.

Frye, Northrop. *The Great Code: The Bible in Literature*. New York: Harcourt Brace Jovanovich, 1982.

Gilbert, Allan H. "Milton and Galileo." *Studies in Philology*, 19 (1922), 152–85.

"Milton's Textbook of Astronomy." *PMLA*, 38 (1923), 297–307.

Gray, John. *The Legacy of Canaan*. 2nd edn. Leiden: E.J. Brill, 1965.

Gunkel, Hermann. *Schöpfung und Chaos in Urzeit und Endzeit*. Göttingen: Vandenhoeck und Ruprecht, 1895.

Hardison, O.B. *The Enduring Monument: A Study of the Idea of Praise in Renaissance Literary Theory and Practice*. Chapel Hill: Univ. of North Carolina Press, 1962.

Works cited

Harris, Victor. *All Coherence Gone*. Chicago: Univ. of Chicago Press, 1949.

Hartman, Geoffrey H. "Milton's Counterplot." *ELH*, 25 (1958), 1–12.
ed. *Psychoanalysis and the Question of the Text*. Baltimore: Johns Hopkins Univ. Press, 1978.

Heidel, Alexander. *The Babylonian Genesis: The Story of Creation*. Chicago: Univ. of Chicago Press, 1951.

Heninger, S. K., Jr. *The Cosmographical Glass: Renaissance Diagrams of the Universe*. San Marino: Huntington Library, 1977.

Hollander, John. *The Untuning of the Sky: Ideas of Music in English Poetry, 1500–1700*. Princeton: Princeton Univ. Press, 1961.

Hughes, Merritt Y. *Ten Perspectives on Milton*. New Haven: Yale Univ. Press, 1965.

Humbert, Paul. "La Relation de Genèse 1 et du Psaume 104 avec la liturgie du Nouvel-An israelite." *Opouscles d'un Hebriasant*. Université de Neuchâtel, 1958.

Hunter, William B., Jr. "Milton Translates the Psalms." *Philological Quarterly*, 40 (1961), 485–94.

Irwin, John T. *Doubling and Incest/Repetition and Revenge: A Speculative Reading of Faulkner*. Baltimore: Johns Hopkins Univ. Press, 1975.

Jacobsen, Thorkild. "Mesopotamia." In *The Intellectual Adventure of Ancient Man*. Ed. H. and H. A. Frankfort. Chicago: Univ. of Chicago Press, 1946, 125–219.

James, E. O. *Myth and Ritual in the Ancient Near East*. New York: Frederick A. Praeger, 1958.

Johnson, Francis R. *Astronomical Thought in Renaissance England*. Baltimore: Johns Hopkins Univ. Press, 1937.

Jones, Richard Foster. *Ancients and Moderns*. St. Louis: Washington Univ. Studies, 1936.

The Seventeenth Century. Stanford: Stanford Univ. Press, 1951.

Kerrigan, William. *The Prophetic Milton*. Charlottesville: Univ. Press of Virginia, 1974.

The Sacred Complex: On the Psychogenesis of "Paradise Lost". Cambridge, Mass.: Harvard Univ. Press, 1983.

Knott, John R., Jr. *The Sword of the Spirit: Puritan Responses to the Bible*. Chicago: Univ. of Chicago Press, 1980.

Kocher, Paul H. *Science and Religion in Elizabethan England*. San Marino: Huntington Library, 1953.

Kristeva, Julia. *The Powers of Horror: An Essay on Abjection*. New York: Columbia Univ. Press, 1982.

Lacan, Jacques. *The Four Fundamental Concepts of Psycho-Analysis*. Ed. Jacques-Alain Miller. Trans. Alan Sheridan. New York: W. W. Norton, 1978.

Laplanche, Jean. *Life and Death in Psychoanalysis*. Trans. Jeffrey Mehlman. Baltimore: Johns Hopkins Univ. Press, 1976.

Levinson, Stephen. *Pragmatics*. Cambridge: Cambridge Univ. Press, 1983.

Lewalski, Barbara K. *Donne's "Anniversaries" and the Poetry of Praise: The Creation of a Symbolic Mode*. Princeton: Princeton Univ. Press, 1973.

Milton's Brief Epic: The Genre, Meaning, and Art of "Paradise Regained." Providence: Brown Univ. Press, 1966.

Works cited

"Paradise Lost" and the Rhetoric of Literary Forms. Princeton: Princeton Univ. Press, 1985.

Protestant Poetics and the Seventeenth-Century Religious Lyric. Princeton: Princeton Univ. Press, 1979.

Lieb, Michael, *The Dialectics of Creation: Patterns of Birth and Regeneration in "Paradise Lost."* Amherst: Univ. of Massachusetts Press, 1970.

"Further Thoughts on Satan's Journey through Chaos." *Milton Quarterly*, 12 (1978), 126–33.

Poetics of the Holy: A Reading of "Paradise Lost." Chapel Hill: Univ. of North Carolina Press, 1981.

Loewald, Hans W. "Some Considerations on Repetition and Repetition Compulsion." *International Journal of Psycho-Analysis*, 52 (1971), 59–66.

Lovejoy, Arthur O. "Milton's Dialogue on Astronomy." In *Reason and the Imagination.* Ed. J. A. Mazzeo. New York: Columbia Univ. Press, 1962.

Luther, Martin. *A Manual of the Book of Psalms.* Trans. Henry Cole. London: 1837.

Martin Luther's Werke: Kritische Gesamtausgabe. Weimar: Bohlau, 1883.

MacCaffrey, Isabel. *Paradise Lost as "Myth."* Cambridge, Mass.: Harvard Univ. Press, 1959.

McColley, Grant. "The Astronomy of *Paradise Lost.*" *Studies in Philology*, 34 (1937), 209–47.

"Milton's Dialogue on Astronomy: The Principle Immediate Sources." *PMLA*, 52 (1937), 728–62.

Malinowski, Bronislaw. *Coral Gardens and Their Magic.* 2 vols. 1935; rpt. New York: Dover, 1978.

Mayerson, Caroline W. "The Orpheus Image in *Lycidas.*" *PMLA*, 64 (1949), 189–207.

Mazzeo, J. A., ed. *Reason and the Imagination: Studies in the History of Ideas 1600–1800.* New York: Columbia Univ. Press, 1962.

Milton, John. *The Complete Prose Works of John Milton.* Ed. Don M. Wolfe et al. 8 vols. New Haven: Yale Univ. Press, 1953–82.

John Milton: Complete Poems and Major Prose. Ed. Merritt Y. Hughes. New York: Odyssey Press, 1957.

Paradise Lost. Ed. Alastair Fowler. London: Longman, 1968.

More, Henry. *An Appendix to the Defense of the Threefold Cabbala.* London, 1713.

Mowinckel, Sigmund. *The Psalms in Israel's Worship.* Trans. D. R. Ap-Thomas. 2 vols. Oxford: Basil Blackwell, 1962.

Nicholson, Marjorie Hope. *The Breaking of the Circle.* Evanston: Northwestern Univ. Press, 1950.

"Milton and the Telescope." *ELH*, 2 (1935), 1–32.

"The 'New Astronomy' and English Literary Imagination." *Studies in Philology*, 32 (1935), 428–62.

Nietzsche, Friedrich. *Thus Spoke Zarathustra.* In *The Portable Nietzsche.* Trans. Walter Kaufman. New York: Viking Press, 1954.

Nohrnberg, James. *The Analogy of the Faerie Queene.* Princeton: Princeton Univ. Press, 1976.

"Moses," in *Images of Man and God: Old Testament Short Stories in Literary Focus.* Ed. Burke O. Long. Sheffield: Almond Press, 1981.

Works cited

Nyquist, Mary. "The Father's Word/Satan's Wrath." *PMLA*, 100, 2 (1985), 187–202.

Patrides, C. A., ed. *The English Poems of George Herbert*. London: J. M. Dent, 1974.

Perkins, Jocelyn. *Westminster Abbey: Its Worship and Ornaments*. 3 vols. London: Oxford Univ. Press, 1938–52.

Plotinus. *The Enneads*. Trans. Stephen MacKenna. 3rd edn., rev. by B. S. Page. London: Faber and Faber, 1962.

Polzin, Robert. *Moses and the Deuteronomist: A Literary Study of the Deuteronomic History*. New York: Seabury Press, 1980.

Pritchard, James B., ed. *Ancient Near Eastern Texts Relating to the Old Testament*. Princeton: Princeton Univ. Press, 1950; 2nd edn., 1955.

Puttenham, George. *The Arte of English Poesie*. 1589. In *Elizabethan Critical Essays*. Ed. George Gregory Smith. London: Oxford Univ. Press, 1904. Vol. 2, 1–193.

Radzinowicz, Mary Ann. *Toward "Samson Agonistes": The Growth of Milton's Mind*. Princeton: Princeton Univ. Press, 1978.

Rank, Otto. *The Double: A Psychoanalytic Study*. Trans. Harry Tucker, Jr. Chapel Hill: Univ. of North Carolina Press, 1971.

Revard, Stella. *The War in Heaven: "Paradise Lost" and the Tradition of Satan's Rebellion*. Ithaca: Cornell Univ. Press, 1980.

Rice, Eugene F., Jr. *The Renaissance Idea of Wisdom*. Cambridge, Mass.: Harvard Univ. Press, 1958.

Ricoeur, Paul. *Freud and Philosophy*. Trans. Denis Savage. New Haven: Yale Univ. Press, 1970.

    The Symbolism of Evil. Trans. Emerson Buchanan. Boston: Beacon Press, 1967.

    Time and Narrative. 2 vols. Trans. Kathleen McLaughlin and David Pellauer. Chicago: Univ. of Chicago Press, 1984.

Ross, Alexander. *The New Planet No Planet: or, The Earth No Wandring Star*. London, 1646.

Said, Edward W. *Beginnings: Intention and Method*. New York: Basic Books, 1975.

Samuel, Irene. "Milton on Learning and Wisdom." *PMLA*, 64 (1949), 708–23.

Sarkar, Malabika. " 'The Visible Diurnal Sphere': Astronomical Images of Space and Time in *Paradise Lost*." *Milton Quarterly*, 18 (1984), 1–5.

Schindler, Walter. *Voice and Crisis: Invocation in Milton's Poetry*. Hamden, Connecticut: Archon Books, 1984.

Scholes, Percy A. *The Puritans and Music in England and New England*. London: Oxford Univ. Press, 1934.

Schultz, Howard. *Milton and Forbidden Knowledge*. New York: Modern Language Assoc., 1955.

Searle, John. "Reiterating the Differences: A Reply to Derrida." *Glyph*, 1 (1977), 198–208.

Shawcross, John T., "*Paradise Lost* and the Theme of the Exodus." *Milton Studies*, 2 (1970), 3–26.

Sidney, Sir Philip. *An Apologie for Poetrie*. 1595. In *Elizabethan Critical Essays*.

Works cited

Ed. George Gregory Smith. London: Oxford Univ. Press, 1904. Vol. 1, 148–207.

Sims, James H. *The Bible in Milton's Epics*. Gainesville: Univ. of Florida Press, 1962.

Sims, James H., and Leland Ryken. *Milton and Scriptural Tradition: The Bible into Poetry*. Columbia: Univ. of Missouri Press, 1984.

Smith, Joseph H. "Rite, Ritual, and Defense." *Psychiatry*, 46 (1983), 16–30.

Soler, Jean. "The Dietary Prohibitions of the Hebrews." Trans. E. Forster. *The New York Review of Books*, 14 June 1979, 24–30.

Speiser, E. A. *Genesis*. Vol. 1 in *The Anchor Bible Series*. Garden City, NY: Doubleday and Co., 1964.

Spitzer, Leo. "Classical and Christian Ideas of World Harmony." *Traditio*, 2 (1944), 409–64; 3 (1945), 307–64. New York: Cosmopolitan Science and Art Service Co., Inc.

Stapleton, Laurence. "Milton and the New Music." *University of Toronto Quarterly*, 23 (1953–54), 217–26.

Stein, Arnold. "Satan's Metamorphoses: The Internal Speech." In vol. 1 of *Milton Studies*. Ed. James D. Simmonds. Pittsburgh: Univ. of Pittsburgh Press, 1969, 93–113.

Stroup, Thomas B. *Religious Rite and Ceremony in Milton's Poetry*. Lexington: Univ. of Kentucky Press, 1968.

Studley, M. H. "Milton and His Paraphrases of the Psalms." *Philological Quarterly*, 4 (1925), 364–72.

Svendsen, Kester. *Milton and Science*. Cambridge, Mass.: Harvard Univ. Press, 1956.

Tayler, Edward W. *Milton's Poetry: Its Development in Time*. Pittsburgh: Duquesne Univ. Press, 1979.

Thorpe, James, ed. *Milton Criticism: Selections from Four Centuries*. New York: Rinehart & Co., Inc., 1950.

Turner, Victor. *The Forest of Symbols: Aspects of Ndembu Ritual*. Ithaca: Cornell Univ. Press, 1967.

van Gennep, Arnold. *The Rites of Passage*. Trans. Monica B. Vizedom and Gabrielle L. Caffee. Chicago: Univ. of Chicago Press, 1960.

von Rad, Gerhard. *Old Testament Theology*. Trans. D. M. G. Stalker. Vols. 1 and 2. New York: Harper and Brothers, 1962–65.

The Problem of the Hexateuch and Other Essays. Trans. E. W. Trueman Dicken. New York: McGraw-Hill, 1966.

Waddington, Raymond B. "Milton Among the Carolines." In *The Age of Milton*. Eds. C. A. Patrides and Raymond B. Waddington. Manchester: Manchester Univ. Press, 1980, 338–64.

Walker, D. P. "Orpheus the Theologian and Renaissance Platonists." *Journal of the Warburg and Courtauld Institutes*, 16 (1953), 100–20.

Watkins, W. B. C. *An Anatomy of Milton's Verse*. Baton Rouge: Louisiana State Univ. Press, 1955.

Werman, Golda Speira. "Midrash in *Paradise Lost: Capitula Rabbi Elieser*." *Milton Studies*, 18 (1983), 145–71.

Westermann, Claus. *A Thousand Years and a Day: Our Time in the Old*

Works cited

Testament. Trans. Stanley Rudman. Philadelphia: Muhlenberg Press, 1962.

Wilkins, Bishop John. *The Discovery of a World in the Moone.* London, 1638; facsimile rpt. New York: Scholars' Facsimiles and Reprints, 1973.

Mathematical and Philosophical Works, 2 vols. London, 1802.

Williams, Arnold. *The Common Expositor: An Account of the Commentaries on Genesis 1527–1633.* Chapel Hill: Univ. of North Carolina Press, 1948.

Wither, George. *A Collection of Emblemes.* London, 1635.

A Preparation to the Psalter. London, 1619; facsimile rpt., Manchester: Charles E. Simms, 1884.

Psalmes of David. Rpt. New York: Burt Franklin, 1967.

Wittreich, Joseph A., Jr. " 'A Poet Among Poets': Milton and the Tradition of Prophecy." In *Milton and the Line of Vision.* Ed. Joseph Wittreich, Jr. Madison: Univ. of Wisconsin Press, 1975.

Visionary Poetics: Milton's Tradition and His Legacy. San Marino: Huntington Library, 1979.

Interpreting "Samson Agonistes." Princeton: Princeton Univ. Press, 1986.

Woodhouse, A. S. P. "Notes on Milton's Early Development." *University of Toronto Quarterly,* 13 (1943–44), 66–101.

"Notes on Milton's Views on the Creation: The Initial Phase." *Philological Quarterly,* 28 (1949), 211–36.

Zacker, Christian K. *Curiosity and Pilgrimage.* Baltimore: Johns Hopkins Univ. Press, 1976.

INDEX

Aaron, 20
Abdiel, 20, 21
Abel, 38
Achilles, 63
Adam, 4, 5, 15, 77–99, 103–09,
    117 n. 2
  aubade of Eve and, 3, 63, 65,
    71–73, 74, 79–80, 84, 89,
    92
  birth of, 54, 56, 67
  despair of, 33, 103–04
  education of, 40–48
  fall of, 3, 39, 92, 113 n. 18
  Michael and, 90, 125 n. 68
  Raphael and, 22, 27, 40–59
    passim
  and redemption, 35, 109
  see also Bible, books of:
    Genesis; Eve; fall, the
Adams, Robert M., 10, 18, 19,
    113 n. 4
Akitu festival, 7, 28, 73, 74, 121
    n. 23
Anaxagoras, 25
Anderson, Bernhard, *Creation
    versus Chaos*, 34
angels, fallen, 2, 19, 20, 45, 53
  in Book of Enoch, 24
  see also Beelzebub; Belial; hell;
    Lucifer; Mammon;
    Moloch; Satan
apocalypse, 27, 29, 30, 32, 34,
    38, 82, 83, 103
  see also Bible, books of:
    Revelation
Apollo, 69

apostrophe, 62
Aristotle, 24, 85, 86
astronomy, 43–47, 59, 116–17
    n. 2
  Augustinian, 50–53
  Copernican, 116–17 n. 2
  Ptolemaic, 116–17 n. 2
  see also Christ, as star; Urania
atomism, 24–26, 114 n. 32, 114–
    15 n. 37
aubade, Adam and Eve's, 3, 63,
    65, 71–74, 79–80, 84, 89,
    92
Augustine, St., 49–53, 105
  Confessions, 50, 81
  Contra Academicos, 118 n. 11
  on curiosity, 54, 118 nn. 17
    and 21
  on evil, 9, 19
  on human will, 104
  on knowledge, 49–53
  on memory, 109–10
  on praise, 50, 81, 83
  on wisdom, 118 n. 11
Austin, J. L., 64, 65, 120 n. 13

Baal, 28
Babel, 38
Barker, Arthur, 81
Beelzebub, 20, 53, 98
Belial, 20, 27
Bellerophon, 59, 60
Benveniste, Emile, 68
Berdjaev, Nicholas, 35
Bible, 1–5, 7, 12, 15, 84–85, 112
    n. 8

Babylonian influence on, 28–29
books of: Genesis, 1, 2, 3, 4, 7, 12, 23, 28, 31, 35, 50, 60, 71, 73, 81, 108, 111 n. 4, 112 n. 6, 121 n. 23, 122 n. 40; Exodus, 2, 3, 4, 29, 64, 73, 111 n. 4; Leviticus, 12, 14, 15, 16, 113 nn. 13 and 18; Numbers, 21; Deuteronomy, 2, 5, 63; Job, 31, 36, 38, 52, 80–81; Psalms, 34, 64, 71, 81, 84, 85, 86, 87, 108, 121 nn. 23 and 27, 123 n. 51, 124 nn. 59 and 61, 125 n. 67; Proverbs, 12, 59, 76; Song of Solomon, 86; Isaiah, 29; II Isaiah, 29; Jeremiah, 76; Amos, 64; Jonah, 34; Zachariah, 31; Mark, 87; Ephesians, 87; Colossians, 87; Hebrews, 103; James, 37, 87; 1 John, 52; Revelation, 27, 64, 72, 86, 115 n. 45, 123 n. 49; "Song of the Sea" *see* Exodus 29
and cosmogonic strife, 27–36
and creation, 81
and dividing, 11
evil in, 34
and memory, 4
and monotheism, 34
and pollution, 14, 15, 16, 17
Blake, William, 6, 8
Bloch, Chana, 123 n. 50
Blumenberg, Hans, 50, 118 nn. 13 and 21
Book of Common Prayer, 75
boundaries
    and chaos, 11–24
    and creation, 11–24
    and Creator, 15
    and diet, 14, 15, 17
    and evil, 12, 13
    between hell and earth, 16
    and identity, 18–24

and knowledge, 41, 52
and locomotion, 15, 16, 17
and the sacred, 11–24
and Satan, 13, 14, 16
and transgression, 13, 14, 15, 16, 17
Burden, Dennis, 90

Cain, 38
Casaubon, Meric, 9, 31
Cassirer, Ernst, 12
Certeau, Michel de, 67
Chalcidius, 24
Chambers, A. B., 10, 11, 23, 24, 114 n. 32
chaos, 1, 6, 7, 8–39
    and atomism, 24, 25
    as Biblical Deep, 23
    vs. creation, 3, 8–39
    epithets of, 19, 23
    evil of, 8–39
    and the fall, 8, 31–39, 92
    as "first matter," 1, 6, 7, 8–39
    God and, 8, 10
    goodness of, 8–39
    and hell, 22–24
    journey through, 26, 27
    and liminality, 11–24
    Milton and, 8–39, 113 n. 4
    neutrality of, 10, 18
    poetry and, 60–90
    and pollution, 17
    and Satan, 10, 13, 18–20
    and theodicy, 11, 31–39
    see also boundaries
Chaos (Anarch), 10, 18, 21–24, 32
Charleton, Walter, 24
Chaucer, Geoffrey, 43
Childs, Brevard, 34
choice, 6–7, 14, 17, 18, 21, 37, 39
Christ, 17, 30–31, 58
    birth of, 78
    passion of, 84, 90
    and praise, 69
    Satan and, 16, 58, 103
    as star, 53

Index

Circe, 90
Coleridge, S. T., 20
Collette, Carolyn, 124 n. 61
confession, 103, 105, 106
cosmogonic conflict, 24–31
    in the Bible, 28–36
    and the fall, 32
Cowley, Abraham, 88
    Davideis, 122 n. 36
creation, 1–59, 115 n. 46
    account by Uriel, 32, 48, 49
    Babylonian account of, 7, 28,
        73, 74, 121 n. 23
    Biblical, 1–7, 28–31, 36, 81
    vs. chaos, 8–39
    de Deo, 9
    denial of, 21, 22
    and dividing, 11
    ex nihilo, 9
    and fall, 22, 31–39, 92
    knowledge of, 40, 53
    poetic, 6, 60–90
    remembered, 22, 72–74,
        79–90
    and repetition, 1–7, 104–10
Cromwell, Oliver, 89
Cross, Frank, Jr., 115 nn. 43 and
    46
Cudworth, Ralph, 25
Culler, Jonathan, 62
curiosity, 49, 50, 118 n. 25
    and knowledge, 40–53
    St. Augustine on, 118 nn. 17
        and 21

Dalila, 114 n. 20
Danielson, Dennis, 32
Dante Alighieri, 43, 93, 105
David, 86–89, 125 n. 68
    see also Bible, books of: Psalms
death, 8, 14, 16, 100–04
death instinct, 93, 94, 100
Death (character), 3, 21, 99, 100,
    101, 102, 103
debt, 66–71, 91
Democritus, 25
Derrida, Jacques, 64, 93, 120 nn.
    13 and 14, 126 n. 7

Dickens, Charles, *Great Expec-
    tations*, 94
dietary law, 14, 15, 16
Discord, 33
diurnal rotation, earth's, 117 n. 2
Donne, John, 87, 93
    An Anatomy of the World, 37
doubling, 99–103, 127 n. 18
Douglas, Mary, 14, 15
    Purity and Danger, 113 n. 16
dualism, 9, 10, 25, 32
Du Bartas, 25, 75

Eden, *see* Paradise
Eliade, Mircea, 74
Empedocles, 25
Empson, William, 23
Enuma Elish, *see* creation,
    Babylonian account of
Epicurus, 25
Erebus, 23
Eros, 93
Eurydice, 89
Eve, 45, 46, 55, 57, 58, 107, 113
    n. 18
    aubade of Adam and, 3, 63,
        71–73, 74, 79–80, 84, 89,
        92
    birth of, 101
    fall of, 3, 15, 38, 61
    guilt of, 105–06
    narcissism and, 100, 101
    penitence of, 65, 72
    suicide wish of, 103–04
    see also Adam; Bible, books of:
        Genesis; fall, the; Paradise;
        Satan
evil
    Augustine on, 9, 10, 19
    cosmological, 8–39
    Milton and, 10
    origin of, 8–39
    Plotinus on, 13
    and theodicy, 17
    see also sin
exhibitionism, 55–58, 119 n. 30
exodus, 1–5, 29, 30, 34
    see also Bible, books of: Exodus

139

Index

fall, the, 32, 45, 92–94, 113–14
    n. 18
  chaos and, 31–39
  see also Adam; Bible, books of:
    Genesis; Eve; Satan
Ficino, 88, 125 n. 70
Fish, Stanley, 31, 120 n. 7
Fixler, Michael, 16, 123 n. 49
flood, the, 38, 62
fort-da game, 97, 126 n. 7
  see also death instinct
Frank, Sebastian, *Forbidden Fruit:
    Or a Treatise on the Tree of
    Knowledge, The*, 113 n. 18
Freer, Coburn, 86
Freud, Sigmund
  and death instinct, 109
  and doubling, 99–100
  "Instincts and Their
    Vicissitudes," 55
  and memory, 109–10
  and narcissism, 99
  and pleasure principle, 92–93,
    100, 126 n. 7
  and repetition compulsion, 6,
    92, 93–103 *passim*, 106,
    127 n. 18
  and scopophilia, 54, 55, 56

Gabriel, 13, 31
gaze, Lacanian, 119 n. 30
genre, 84–87, 91
Gnosticism, 8, 116 n. 57
God, 3, 4, 6, 12, 36, 111 n. 4
  and chaos, 8, 10
  and creation, 12, 14, 22
  knowledge of, 45
  sadism of, 57, 116 n. 1
  and Satan, 18, 26, 30
  see also Adam; Bible; Christ;
    creation; Eve; heaven;
    Paradise
Goodman, Godfrey, *Fall of Man
    or the Corruption of Nature,
    The*, 37
Goodwin, Thomas, 33
Gunkel, Hermann, 121 n. 23

Hades (consort of Chaos), 23
  see also hell
Hakewill, George, *Apology of the
    Power and Providence of God,
    An*, 37
Hardison, O. B., 85
Hartman, Geoffrey, 3
heaven, 12, 23
  war in, 3, 26–28, 29, 34, 38
  see also angels, fallen; God;
    Satan
Hecate, 23
hell, 14, 19, 20, 23
  and chaos, 22–24
  debate in, 20, 53–54, 98
  devils' song in, 89–90
  and Satan, 24, 96
  see also angels, fallen; heaven,
    war in; Satan
Heninger, S. K., Jr., 114 n. 37
Herbert, George
  "Easter," 84
  "Providence," 69
  The Temple, 123 n. 50
Hollander, John, 77
Hollar, Wenceslaus, 114 n. 37
Humbert, Paul, 121 n. 23
hymn
  and "Nativity Ode," 79–83
  Paradise Lost as, 63–66, 83–90

Ibn Ezra, 113 n. 9
interpretation, 6, 60–66
invocations, in *Paradise Lost*, 62,
    63
  to Book I, 60, 61, 84
  to Book III, 56–59, 61,
    107–10
  to Book VII, 61–63
Israel, 2, 5, 12, 29, 64, 112 n. 5
  dietary laws of, 14

Jerusalem, 12
Job, 36, 80–81, 86, 88
  see also Bible, books of: Job;
    Leviathan
Johnson, Samuel, 63, 99, 123
    n. 48

Index

Jonah, 34
  see also Bible, books of: Jonah

Kerrigan, William, 119 n. 32
Kierkegaard, Sóren, 110
Knott, John R., Jr., 120 n. 11
knowledge, 6, 40–53, 58, 59, 118
  n. 13
  boundaries of, 40–53
  curiosity and, 41–54
  food and, 4, 42
  of God, 45
  and pragmatism, 44–47
  praise and, 48–49
  Satanic, 53–54
  scopophilia and, 54–59
Knox, Ronald, 113 n. 13
Korah, rebellion of, 20–21
  see also Bible, books of:
    Numbers
Kristeva, Julia, 17

Lacan, Jacques, 119 n. 30
Laplanche, Jean, 93
Lavinia, 63
Lefèvre de la Boderie, Guy, 88
Levi, sons of, 20
Leviathan, 23, 29, 31, 36, 115
  n. 45
Lewalski, Barbara K., 84, 87, 124
  n. 59
Lieb, Michael, 10, 113–14 n. 18
liminality, 18–20, 99
  see also chaos
liturgy, 75, 76, 83–90
  as cosmic harmony, 77–83
  creation and, 73–78, 84
  see also hymn; ritual
Loewald, Hans, 105, 106, 110
loss, 91, 92, 108–10
Lotan, 115 n. 45
Lovejoy, Arthur O., 44, 52, 116
  n. 1
Lucifer, 52, 71
Lucretius, 25
Luther, Martin, 64, 87

MacCaffrey, Isabel, 27

Paradise Lost as "Myth," 114
  n. 31
McColley, Grant, 116 n. 2
McMullen, Chester, 119 n. 33
Malinowksi, Bronislaw, 63
Mammon, 54
Manicheans, 50, 51, 116 n. 57
Marduk, 28
Marot, Clémont, *Pseaumes*, 88
Marvell, Andrew, 88
memory, *see* remembering
Methodius, *Concerning Free Will*, 36
Michael, 3, 62, 90, 125 n. 68
Milton, John
  astronomy of, 44, 46, 59,
    116–17 n. 1
  and atomism, 114 n. 32
  blindness of, 51, 56, 59, 109
  and chaos, 8–39, 113 n. 4
  and creation, 8–39, 40–41
  and David, 88, 125 n. 68
  on good and evil, 10, 37
  and liturgy, 74–78, 84
  as monist, 9, 10
  and Orpheus, 88–90, 125
    n. 73
  Puritanism of, 75–76
  works of: *Ad Patrem*, 5, 66–72
    passim, 89; *Arcades*, 79;
    Apology for Smectymnuus, 75;
    Areopagitica, 6, 37, 43; *At a
    Solemn Music*, 76, 79, 82; *At
    a Vacation Exercise*, 45, 58;
    Comus, 65, 90; *De Doctrina
    Christiana*, 4, 10, 11, 19, 76;
    Defensio Secunda, 5, 51, 69;
    Eikonoclastes, 75; *L'Allegro*,
    89; *Lycidas*, 72, 83, 89, 103,
    115 n. 40; *Naturam Non Pati
    Senium*, 37, 38; *Of Education*,
    44, 47; *On the Morning of
    Christ's Nativity*, 70, 78–84
    passim; *Paradise Regained*, 16,
    58, 69, 80, 86, 125 n. 68;
    Passion, The, 82, 90; *Reason
    of Church Government, The*,
    86; *Samson Agonistes*, 65, 114
    n. 20, 123 n. 51; *Second*

Index

Defense ..., *see Defensio Secunda; Second Prolusion*, 76, 77; *Seventh Prolusion*, 45, 47, 89; *Sixth Elegy*, 79, 89; *Upon the Circumcision*, 82
see also Paradise Lost
Moloch, 20, 98–99
monism, 9, 10
More, Henry, 18, 25
Moses, 4, 5, 12, 20, 21, 43
see also Bible, books of: Exodus, Deuteronomy
music, *see* aubade; hymn; liturgy; song
music of the spheres, 76–83
myth, 28
 Babylonian, 7, 28, 115 n. 45
 Canaanite, 115 n. 45
 Ugaritic, 28, 115 nn. 43–45

narcissism, 99–102
 of Eve, 100, 101
 of Satan, 100
 see also doubling
Neoplatonism, 10
Nietzsche, Friedrich, 95–96, 126 n. 11
No-Address Resolution, 124 n. 61

Orcus, 23
Ordinance for the Suppression of Blasphemie and Heresies, 124 n. 61
origins, 1, 2, 40–59, 117 n. 8
Orpheus, 60, 62, 88–90, 125 nn. 70 and 73
 see also Eurydice
Ovid, 23
 Metamorphoses, 70

Pandemonium, 97
Paradise, 13, 15, 33, 34, 46
 departure of Adam and Eve from, 39
 Satan's plot for 54, 55, 65
 see also Adam; Bible, books of: Genesis; Eve; fall, the; Satan

Paradise Lost
 cosmogonic conflict in, 28–31
 debate in hell, 97–99
 as hymn, 63–66, 83–90
 invocation, *see* invocations
 Book I, 2, 10, 19, 20, 23, 35, 36, 54, 56, 59, 60, 81, 94, 95–99, 110
 Book II, 2, 12, 13, 17–20, 23, 24, 26, 27, 53, 54, 61, 65, 70, 89–90, 96, 98–102
 Book III, 2, 17, 30, 32, 40, 47, 48, 56–58, 61, 82–83, 108, 109
 Book IV, 13, 24, 27, 46, 54–56, 58, 65–68, 91, 96, 97, 100, 101, 105, 107, 109
 Book V, 5, 8, 13, 21, 22, 40, 41, 42, 71–72, 74, 84, 107
 Book VI, 2, 5, 16, 26, 27
 Book VII, 4, 11, 22, 26, 30, 31, 35, 40, 42, 48, 56–58, 61, 62–64, 73, 74, 78, 89
 Book VIII, 42, 44, 45, 47, 49, 54–55
 Book IX, 2, 15, 16, 56, 61, 63, 65, 96, 97, 99
 Book X, 15, 16, 33, 61, 85, 101, 103–06
 Book XI, 39, 104
 Book XII, 35, 39, 59, 104, 108
Paradise of Fools, 17
Passover, 3
Paul, St., 49
penance, 105
performative utterance, 6, 60–66, 80, 85
Phaethon, 70
Pharaoh, 29
Phlegethon, 23
Pico della Mirandola, 88, 125 n. 70
Plato, 12, 49, 76, 85, 86, 114 n. 32
pleasure principle, *see* Freud
Plotinus, 13
praise, 47–49

Index

hymns of, 63–65, 66–90, 91, 108–10
  knowledge and, 47–49, 58–59
  Satan and, 47, 65, 66, 67, 70
Preston, John, 64
Priestly writer, 3, 12, 63, 73, 112 n. 6
Prometheus, 76, 77
Prynne, William, 75, 76
psalms, as genre, 84–90, 91
psalter, national, 88, 125 n. 67
Pseudepigrapha: a Book of Enoch, 23, 24
Puttenham, George, *Arte of English Poesie, The*, 86
Pythagorians, 12, 76, 77

Radzinowicz, Mary Ann, 87, 124 n. 61
  Toward "Samson Agonistes", 123 n. 51
Rahab, 29
Rank, Otto, 99, 100, 102
Raphael, 1, 3, 9, 22, 30, 54
  educating Adam, 5, 27, 40–61 *passim*, 78, 79
Rashi, 12
re-creation, 3, 6, 38, 39
  see also creation; repetition
redemption, 2, 32, 35, 36, 119 n. 33
  see also apocalypse
Red Sea, 2, 29
remembering, 3–7
  and creation, 14, 15
  in hymn, 60–90, 91, 92, 94, 106–10
repetition, 1–7, 91–110 *passim*, 127 n. 18
  and chaos, 38, 91–93
  compulsion, 6, 92, 93, 94–103, 104–10, 127 n. 18
  cosmogonic, 5–7
  and creation, 38, 39, 91–93, 104–10
  and ritual, 3–7, 82–83, 91–94
revenge, 96–98, 99, 110

Rice, Eugene, 118 n. 13
Ricoeur, Paul, 30, 32, 33, 73, 92, 93, 106, 109, 121 n. 23, 126 n. 2
rites of passage, 18
ritual, 73–90, 91, 92, 94, 109–10
  see also hymn; liturgy

sabbath, 3–4, 6, 39, 73–74, 75
sadism, 54, 55, 116 n. 1
Said, Edward, 1, 92
Salmasius, 109
Samson, 14
Samuel, Irene, 52, 116 n. 1
Satan, 3–11 *passim*, 14–17, 23, 24, 26, 27, 33, 44–49 *passim*, 57, 90, 93, 94
  and chaos, 16–20, 22, 26
  and Christ, 16, 58, 103
  and curiosity, 51
  and debate in hell, 20, 54
  as enemy of God, 26, 30, 61
  fall of, 13, 19–21, 92, 95–96
  narcissism of, 100
  and praise, 67–68, 70, 83
  "repentance" of, 65–67, 68
  and revenge, 96–98, 99, 110
  as serpent, 5, 15–16, 55, 65
  Uriel and, 55, 57
  will of, 94–103
  see also Adam; angels, fallen; Bible, books of: Genesis, Revelation; Eve; fall, the; heaven, war in; hell; Paradise
Saul, 88
Scholasticism, 50
Schultz, Howard, 50
scopophilia, 54–59 *passim*, 119 nn. 30 and 33
Seneca, 23, 49
Sheol, 23, 34
Sidney, Sir Philip, 86, 88, 124 n. 56
sin, 32, 33, 43
  see also evil; fall, the
Sin (character), 3, 21, 53, 54, 99, 100, 101, 102

143

Index

and Death, allegory of,
99–103
see also Death (character)
Sinai, 4, 23, 82
Soler, Jean, 14
song, sacred, 6, 60–90
see also hymn
Spenser, Edmund, 27
Spitzer, Leo, 77
Stapleton, Laurence, 122 n. 32
Statius, 23, 70
Stein, Arnold, 26
Stoicism, 49
Stroup, Thomas B., 123 n. 49

Tabernacles, Feast of, 121 n. 23
Tayler, Edward W., 81–82
Thales, 50, 59
thanatophobia, 102, 103
Tiamat (and Tehom), 7, 28, 29,
31
time, 94–97
Turner, Victor, 18
typology, 82

Urania, 49, 59
Uriel, 1, 3, 30, 32, 47–48, 49, 53
Satan and, 55, 57

Valentinianism, 36, 37
van Gennep, Arnold, 18
Vicars, John, 75
Virgil, 23
von Rad, Gerhard, 2, 111 n. 4,
112 n. 5
voyeurism, *see* scopophilia

Waddington, Raymond B., 85,
87
war
and chaos, 26–31
in heaven, 20
Watkins, W. B. C., 22
Westermann, Claus, 111 n. 4, 122
n. 4
Wilde, Oscar, *Picture of Dorian
Gray, The*, 100, 102
Wilkins, John, 117 n. 2
will, Satanic, 94–103
wisdom, *see* knowledge
Wisdom (sister of Urania), 59
Wither, George, 49, 78, 86
Woodhouse, A. S. P., 10, 11, 36,
81

Yamm, 28, 115 n. 45

144